CONCISE
LINCOLN
LIBRARY

EDITED BY RICHARD W. ETULAIN
AND SYLVIA FRANK RODRIGUE

JASON H. SILVERMAN

Lincoln and the Immigrant

Southern Illinois University Press
Carbondale

18 17 16 15   4 3 2 1

The Concise Lincoln Library has been made possible
in part through a generous donation by the Leland E.
and LaRita R. Boren Trust.

Jacket illustration adapted from a painting by
Wendy Allen

Library of Congress Cataloging-in-Publication Data
Silverman, Jason H.
Lincoln and the immigrant / Jason H. Silverman.
    pages cm. — (Concise Lincoln library)
Includes bibliographical references and index.
ISBN 978-0-8093-3434-6 (cloth : alk. paper)
ISBN 0-8093-3434-8 (cloth : alk. paper)
ISBN 978-0-8093-3435-3 (e-book)
ISBN 0-8093-3435-6 (e-book)
1. Lincoln, Abraham, 1809–1865—Relations with
immigrants. 2. Lincoln, Abraham, 1809–1865—
Political and social views. 3. United States—
Emigration and immigration—History—19th
century. 4. Immigrants—United States—History
—19th century. I. Title.
E457.2.S56 2015
325.7309'034—dc23   2014047733

Printed on recycled paper. ♻
The paper used in this publication meets the minimum
requirements of American National Standard for Information Sciences—Permanence of Paper for Printed
Library Materials, ANSI Z39.48-1992. ∞

Omnes alumni mei elitr Winthrop

Die when I may, I want it said of me by those who knew me best, to say that I always plucked a thistle and planted a flower where I thought a flower would grow.

—Abraham Lincoln

CONTENTS

Gallery of illustrations beginning on page 53

LINCOLN AND THE IMMIGRANT

INTRODUCTION

"Another Lincoln book?" asked the gentleman sitting next to me on the train from Springfield to Chicago. "Can anything *really* new be said about the guy?" Having just left the Abraham Lincoln Library and Presidential Museum, I was certainly prepared to tell him yes, most definitely. But, his point was well taken. As early as 1934, the legendary Lincoln scholar James G. Randall, in a well-known article, asked, "Has the Lincoln theme been exhausted?" He noted the many then unexplored fields of unedited works, the topics and themes that had not yet been examined, and concluded optimistically that despite a list of some three thousand works at that time, great progress was still possible in the field of Lincoln studies. Others who followed were not as sanguine. In an essay written in 1960 during the centennial celebration of Lincoln's election, one scholar said wryly, "We know more about Lincoln's day-by-day activity than he knew; we know more about his family and ancestors than he knew. Some of our scholars know more about the details of his life than they know of their own."[1] Despite this acerbic view, Lincoln remained as mysterious as ever, and the paths to new interpretations remained potentially open.

If that attitude was present more than half a century ago, then what about now? For just as the Illinois countryside passed by our Amtrak window, a tower was being constructed outside the foyer of the new Ford's Theatre Center for Education and Leadership in Washington, DC. Arising from the floor, it ascended to thirty-four feet, more than three stories high, and was built of sixty-eight hundred aluminum facsimile books. The tower symbolically represented some sixteen thousand titles and counting, more than five times what existed when Randall wrote his essay. This was the work of many lifetimes, all devoted to a single life, that of Abraham Lincoln, the humble rail-splitter from the town I had just visited. Almost six thousand biographies alone have been written of Lincoln, compared with half that number of George Washington. Were one to read all of those Lincoln books, it could easily take a lifetime as well. And yet there was not one book in the tower on the simple subject that I had been researching in Springfield: the relationship of Abraham Lincoln to the immigrant. This would seem to verify the center's belief that its tower "symbolized that the last word about this great man will never be written."[2] It was with pleasure, and with a smile, that I turned to my traveling companion and responded, "Why, yes indeed, something new can be said about Abraham Lincoln."

At one time the Library of Congress estimated that a book on Abraham Lincoln was published every five and a half days. Since the bicentennial of Lincoln's birth, celebrated in 2009, that rate likely increased. Even so, there has not yet been a book-length study devoted to Lincoln and the immigrant. Scores of volumes have been published on Lincoln's philosophy about race, with but a few scholars acknowledging the connection to Lincoln's very serious and significant thoughts about the immigrant and ethnicity. However, Lincoln spent a considerable amount of time pondering the future and place of immigrants in American society, and studying his thoughts on this subject can inform and edify us on his views on slavery and freedom as well.

Little of what he said about immigrants has ever made it into the history books, including those books specifically about Abraham Lincoln. However, there is most assuredly a connection between Lincoln's views on slavery and his long-held beliefs about immigration, and we can gain some valuable and revealing insights by examining the sixteenth president's views on the immigrant in American society.[3]

Abraham Lincoln and immigration? Absolutely. Lincoln lived in an era when immigration was as controversial as it is today. During the twenty years before the Civil War, more than four million immigrants, mostly from Ireland, Germany, and Scandinavia, entered the United States. Additionally, many migrated across the newly defined Mexican border. Processing procedures at such ports as New York's Castle Garden were inconsistent and inhumane. As millions of Catholics arrived, it struck fear in many American Protestants. Consequently, in the 1850s nativist anti-Catholicism cropped up around the country in popular literature featuring stereotypes and supporting the politics of the anti-immigrant Know Nothing, or American, Party. While they were not serious contenders for national political power, many Know Nothing governors, mayors, and congressmen built their careers on opposing immigration.

From an early age, however, Lincoln developed awareness and a tolerance for different peoples and their cultures. While no doubt a product of his time, Lincoln nevertheless refused to let his environment blind him to the strengths of diversity, and throughout his legal and political career he retained an affinity for immigrants, especially the Germans, Irish, Jews, and Scandinavians. His travels at a young age down the Mississippi River to the port of New Orleans exposed him to the sights, sounds, and tastes of a world he hitherto only could have dreamed about. More important, however, it established a foundation for his beliefs and a sympathy that he retained for the rest of his life when it came to the foreign-born, as well as the enslaved.

It recently has been discovered that during his less-than-successful single term in the US House of Representatives, Lincoln joined many other Americans in making a contribution of $10 ($500 in today's money) to the Irish Relief Fund during the Great Famine. Perhaps this was because Lincoln's first teacher at Riney's School in Hodgenville, Hardin County, Kentucky, had been of Irish descent. Master Zachariah Riney was described as "a man of excellent character, deep piety and fair education. He had been reared a Catholic, but made no attempt to proselyte . . . and the great President always mentioned him in terms of grateful respect." Whether Riney left a lasting impression on him or not, Lincoln was always interested in Irish culture. He knew and recited Robert Emmet's "Speech from the Dock," especially the closing words: "Let no man write my epitaph; for as no man who knows my motives dare now vindicate them, let not prejudice or ignorance, asperse them. . . . When my country takes her place among the nations of the earth, *then and not till then*, let my epitaph be written. I have done." Lincoln's favorite ballad was a poem by Helen Selina, Lady Dufferin, titled "The Lament of the Irish Emigrant," set to music.[4]

While many of Lincoln's quips are famous, he often resorted to Irish analogies, sometimes caustic and perhaps a bit insulting, to make his point. Lincoln's first recorded jibe about a poor Irishman comes from one of his congressional speeches on the need for sensible internal improvements, when he described the plight of a man with new boots: "'I shall niver git 'em on,' says Patrick 'till I wear 'em a day or two, and stretch 'em a little.'" Late in the war, one contemporary observer of Lincoln recalled a cabinet meeting when "something was said about hunting up 'Jeff Davis,' and Mr. Lincoln said he hoped 'he would be like Paddy's flea,' when they got their fingers on him he would not be there." This comment is quite consistent with Lincoln's desire to avoid show trials or punitive commissions. Wanting reconciliation, Lincoln used jokes, oftentimes ethnic ones, to soften a message of mercy or conceal a willful blindness to past wrongs. But these jests were not very racist or harsh, certainly not when compared with those of his contemporaries. Both show sympathy and awareness for the poor man's plight, chiding him mildly for his poverty and traditions. Doubtless in that day, nearly everyone, most especially poor immigrants, understood the problems of fleas and ill-fitting footwear.[5]

When the Republican Party was formed in 1854, some Know Nothings drifted into the new party and wanted Republicans to adopt an anti-immigrant stand. Lincoln refused. When he ran for president, Lincoln opposed any change in the naturalization laws or any state legislation by which the rights of citizenship that had previously been accorded to immigrants from foreign lands would be abridged or impaired. He advocated that a full and efficient protection of the rights of all classes of citizens, whether native or naturalized, both at home and abroad, be guaranteed.

Throughout his life Lincoln was closer to no other immigrant group than the Germans who marched with him all the way to the White House. Although some question today whether German support was as responsible for Lincoln's 1860 election as previously believed, Germans nevertheless provided significant support and were effusive in their praise of him. And Lincoln enjoyed the Germans and their culture.

While visiting Cincinnati on his way to Washington, the president-elect was in his hotel room one night when outside a group of German workingmen came to serenade him. "Mr. Lincoln had put off the melancholy mood that appeared to control him during the day," observed Cincinnati resident William Henry Smith, "and was entertaining those [Germans] present with genial, even lively conversation." Lincoln went to his balcony to find nearly two thousand more "of the substantial German citizens who had voted for [him] because they believed him to be a stout champion of free labor and free homesteads."

Lincoln listened attentively as Frederick Oberkleine spoke for his countrymen. "We, the German free workingmen of Cincinnati, avail ourselves of this opportunity to assure you," Oberkleine said to Lincoln, "our chosen Chief Magistrate, of our sincere and heartfelt regard. You earned our votes as the champion of Free Labor and Free Homesteads. Our vanquished opponents have, in recent times, made frequent use of the terms 'Workingmen' and 'Workingmen's Meetings,' in order to create an impression that the mass of workingmen were *in favor of compromises between the interests of free labor and slave labor, by which the victory just won would be turned into a defeat.* This is the despicable device of dishonest men. We spurn such compromises. *We firmly adhere to the principles which directed our votes in your favor. We trust that you, the self-reliant because [you are a] self-made man, will uphold the Constitution and the laws against such treachery and avowed treason.* If to this end you should be in need of men, the German free workingmen, with others, will rise as one man at your call, ready to risk their lives in the effort to maintain the victory already won by freedom over slavery."[6] It would soon prove that the Germans surely delivered on their promise.

The immigrant in Lincoln's economic vision of free soil and free labor, while woven throughout Lincoln studies, has seldom been explored on its own. And yet the well-being of the immigrant was very important to him. Lincoln understood the challenges that immigrants faced in both rural and urban America. He had worked the land with his own hands for fifteen years, surveyed it for five, and spent nine-tenths of his life in agricultural areas. As a lawyer practicing land law at times and as a politician representing a rural district, he had to pay attention to the national debate over the future of public lands, to issues linked to real estate taxes, to the relationship between town and country, and to the importance of the foreign-born as their presence increased in the American labor force.[7]

In more than three decades of public life Lincoln probably talked more about economics, broadly defined, than any other issue, slavery included. The bulk of his discussions with an economic focus preceded the period of his fame. But the core of his thinking in this regard, and readily applicable to the growing immigrant population in his day, was an intense and continually developing commitment to the ideal that all people should receive a full and fair reward for their labors so that they might have the opportunity to rise in life. For the son of an almost illiterate, poor father, a son who in time rose to the White House, this commitment was also a personal one. And this, Lincoln's American Dream, became a mantra and remained so throughout his entire political life.[8]

Lincoln possessed sympathy for "the many poor," as he called them, since he himself had long been one. By the 1850s his compassion manifested in a full-blown ideology of supporting those governmental policies aimed at economic development and free labor, including welcoming, accepting, and using immigrant labor. Lincoln fully understood that such development enhanced the chances that the common people would improve their lives.

One such manifestation of Lincoln's broad view of how best to serve the interests of "the many poor" was his attitude toward immigrants. He never shared the nativist leanings of the old Whigs. Certainly his attitude had a political ingredient to it, but it was also made up much more of future hopes than of contemporary realities. Few immigrants appear to have been attracted to his party until it became Republican. Much more crucial were his central economic beliefs. On the one hand, he bade "God speed" to the immigrants if they could improve their lot by leaving their homes and coming to America; on the other hand, he identified, correctly for his time and place, the growth of population, native and foreign-born, with economic development. Although his humane approach stopped short of that of one of his economic advisors, Henry Charles Carey, who crassly valued immigrants at $1,000 a head and declared that men are "better than gold," Lincoln, too, saw immigrants as important—the most important of any country's "natural resources."[9]

The Civil War not only diverted thousands of Americans from civilian to military pursuits but also drastically reduced immigration. At first the Lincoln administration tried to confront the situation through unofficial State Department efforts and by aiding the work of state agents. But by the end of 1863 Lincoln decided to do more and directly asked Congress for assistance. His annual message to Congress that year requested that it devise a system for encouraging immigration. He spoke of the flow of immigrants from the Old World as a "source of national wealth" and pointed to the labor shortage in both agriculture and industry and to the "tens of thousands of persons, destitute of remunerative occupation," who desired to come to America but needed assistance to do so. His conclusion showed that in spite of slavery and the war, Lincoln could still be a perceptive observer of the American need for immigrant labor. It was in such context that he said, "It is easy to see that, under the sharp discipline of civil war, the nation is beginning a new life. This noble effort demands the aid, and ought to receive the attention and support of the government." Congress responded favorably to the presidential request, and in time immigrants contributed in a major way to the advent of the American industrial revolution, "beginning a new life" not only for themselves but also for their adopted country.[10]

Whereas industrialists and American laborers could be quite unfriendly to the idea of governmental assistance to immigrants, Lincoln saw no inconsistency between his devotion to the workingmen and his support of immigration. He was certain that mineral discoveries and the Homestead Act, giving government-owned land to those who would settle in the West, would attract thousands of men from home and abroad and provide ample opportunity for all. For America and for Lincoln, with the economy ever growing, the problem was not a glut on the labor market—quite the opposite. To Abraham Lincoln, the immigrant deserved a fair chance in America, and he did what he could to ensure that, despite the many distractions he faced.

To his dying day, Lincoln related to the immigrant in a manner that few of his contemporaries would or could. During one of his early speeches, Lincoln regaled the audience with his memory of working on a flatboat for eight dollars a month and having but one pair of buckskin breeches to his name. "Now if you know the nature of buckskin when wet and dried by the sun," Lincoln reminisced, "it will shrink; and my breeches kept shrinking until they left several inches of my legs bare between the tops of my socks and the lower part of my breeches; and whilst I was growing taller they were becoming shorter, and so much tighter that they left a blue streak around my legs that can be seen to this day. If you call this aristocracy I plead guilty to the charge." Not many people could doubt where Lincoln's allegiance lay. More than a few immigrants could relate to Lincoln's stories of poverty and austerity. He was of the people, the common man, the immigrant, whom Lincoln said God loved so much because He made so many of them.[11]

To Lincoln, America never ceased to be the land of opportunity, and he welcomed newcomers to its shores long before the Statue of Liberty represented the immortal words of Emma Lazarus. Early in 1861, on his way to Washington, Lincoln spoke in Trenton, New Jersey, about the Revolutionary War and the battle there in which George Washington had defeated the Hessians. His thoughts drifted back to his first childhood readings in history. "You all know," he said to the New Jersey Senate, "for you have all been boys, how these early impressions last longer than any others. I recollect thinking then, boy even though I was, that there must have been something more than common that those men struggled for. I am exceedingly anxious that that thing which they struggled for; that something even more than National Independence; that something that held out a great promise to all the people of the world to all time to come; I am exceedingly anxious that this Union, the Constitution, and the liberties of the people shall be perpetuated in accordance with the original ideal for which the struggle was made, and I shall be most happy indeed if I shall be an humble instrument in the hands of the Almighty, and of this, his almost chosen people, for perpetuating the object of that great struggle."

That struggle, to Lincoln, created a nation in which a poor, backwoods boy could rise to the pinnacles of power and success. It had allowed him to do so, and he sought to ensure that others, regardless of their nationality, would have the same chance. The feelings born from remembering his past were evident several days later when, in another speech, Lincoln "with deep emotion" presented his political philosophy in but two sentences: "I have never had a feeling politically that did not spring from the sentiments embodied in the Declaration of Independence. . . . It was that which gave promise that in due time the weights should be lifted from the shoulders of all men, and that all should have an equal chance."[12]

This, then, is the story of the decidedly humble, unaristocratic Abraham Lincoln and his personal, professional, and political relationship with the immigrant. It all began with a poor boy's conviction that people should receive the full fruit of their labor so that they might get ahead in life. The conviction matured slowly, over decades. And as Lincoln stood on the threshold of the White house, his convictions had become unshakable. The United States had to be saved with the dream of American promise intact.

Studying Lincoln, however, is all too frequently an exercise in frustration. He kept no diary, no journal, and his private thoughts to himself. Other than his letters, legal papers, and a brief campaign autobiography, the historian is left with only the recollections of those closest to him, such as his son Robert; his cousin John Hanks, who accompanied him on his trips to New Orleans; his law partner, William Herndon; his presidential secretaries, John Hay, John Nicolay, and William O. Stoddard; cabinet members such as diarist Gideon Welles; and prominent immigrant leaders, including Gustave Koerner and Carl Schurz. Newspapers fill in some of the gaps with coverage of Lincoln's speeches and activities, although one must never forget how intensely politicized they were. And there is precious little on Lincoln's relationship with French, Italian, Canadian,

English, and eastern European immigrants; hence I have been unable to include them herein.

Still, for over three decades as a university professor I have preached to my students the efficacy and sacrosanctity of primary source documents. With that in mind, I have allowed Lincoln and his contemporaries to speak for themselves, sometimes at length, throughout this study, believing, as I have throughout my career, that to paraphrase is often to disrespect, if not unnecessarily modernize. I have tried to give Lincoln flesh and blood by exploring his human reactions to the world in which he lived through the power of his words. For that is how you learn to appreciate his greatness even more. That is what history is all about. To read the words from Lincoln and his time is to thrillingly eavesdrop on a world far removed from our own. It is also to see firsthand how Lincoln grappled with the myriad issues that confronted him, including the place of the immigrant in American society and economy.

Often when he was in the Telegraph Office, pacing or pondering, Lincoln would say to the awestruck soldiers as he prepared to leave, "Well, boys, I am down to the raisins," a phrase from one of his many stories, meaning he was finished for the night and had completed his task.[13] It is my hope that by expanding the horizon of Lincoln studies to include his relationship with the immigrants, we will come that much closer to getting "down to the raisins" in figuring out just who was this enigma called Abraham Lincoln.

UNCERTAINTY: A CLASH OF IMAGES

It must have been an odd sight indeed for anyone who saw the tall, lanky boy and his companions sailing down the Mississippi River on a raft with a log cabin, barrels, and hogs, the young Lincoln looking wide-eyed and in awe of everything he saw. Just twenty years old and finally freed of his obligations to his father and the family farm, Lincoln set off in 1828 from Sangamon County, Illinois, on an adventure of a lifetime—a flatboat journey with his stepbrother John Johnston, cousin John Hanks, and employer Dennis Offutt. For the first time in his young life, Abraham Lincoln was traveling afar, and what he would see would shape his thoughts for the remainder of his life. During this trip, Lincoln would first come in contact with foreigners in the exotic port city of New Orleans. And although he probably "did not distinguish Swedes from the Dutchmen, Italians, Spaniards, Swiss, Norwegians, and Russians whom he encountered on the streets and wharves of the cosmopolitan city," he did come to understand for the first time in his life that immigrants from many lands formed part of the American population.[1]

Lincoln's two flatboat voyages to New Orleans were exceptionally important in his development. They represented his only sojourns into the Deep South, exposing him to the institutions of slavery and slave trading. And his experiences during these first visits to a major city were the closest he ever came to being immersed in a foreign culture.

Lincoln did not write or speak of his trips save for brief descriptions of the preparations and a couple of incidents in Illinois. But others did. Lincoln's eventual law partner and biographer, William Herndon, interviewed John Hanks, who had joined Lincoln on his second trip to New Orleans, departing from Illinois in 1831. Hanks, the cousin of Lincoln's biological mother, told Herndon, "In May we landed in N.O. There it was we Saw Negroes Chained—mal-treated—whipt & scourged. Lincoln Saw it—his heart bled—Said nothing much—was silent from feeling—was Sad—looked bad—felt bad—was thoughtful & abstracted—I Can say Knowingly that it was on this trip that he formed his opinions . . . it ran its iron in him then & there—May 1831. I have heard him say—often & often."[2]

Lincoln's two flatboat journeys provided him with firsthand knowl-edge of the country's vastness. None of his subsequent travels would ever match them in length. His river experiences of 1826–32, particu-larly the New Orleans trips of 1828 and 1831, introduced him to the great potential of long-distance commerce and the shortcomings of America's existing modes of transportation. To Lincoln, the solution was the popularly known policy of "internal improvements," such as navigable rivers, bridges, canals, roads, and railroads.

Indeed, Lincoln's first public-policy speech, delivered two years after his first New Orleans trip, emphasized internal improvements for central Illinois. And while seeking a seat in the Illinois state legislature within a year after his second New Orleans trip, Lincoln promoted improved navigability of the Sangamon River as part of his platform.

Lincoln understood and preached that a better transportation system would improve the economic life of Illinoisans, raising liv-ing standards for all and enhancing property values. Lincoln's river journeys also illustrated to him that by controlling the unsettled domains in Illinois, the state could accelerate immigration. It is un-derstandable that wealth and population were practically synony-mous for Lincoln, residing as he did in a sparsely populated region. Immigrants would bring economic growth and all that it implied. Indeed, seeing America firsthand from a flatboat at a young age in-stilled in Lincoln core Whig social and economic philosophies such as free labor, transportation modernization, internal improvements, and most assuredly, the need to attract immigration.[3]

Lincoln's trips to New Orleans represented his only journeys deep into the slave South, where enslaved African Americans not only abounded but overwhelmingly predominated. New Orleans also ranked as the largest city the young Lincoln had ever seen, and this remained the case until he stepped onto the national stage as a newly elected congressman in 1848. More important, it was the most ethnically and culturally diverse city in the United States in the early nineteenth century. Although Lincoln later took a day trip to Niagara Falls, Canada, in 1857, New Orleans was the closest he ever came to entering an international city. And while Lincoln occasionally encountered French- or Spanish-speaking immigrants or Catholics in his early years in Indiana, Illinois, and on the Ohio River, his trips to New Orleans immersed him in a variety of different cultures, races, ethnicities, ancestries, religions, languages, classes, cuisines, and architectures. All this plus its sheer urban size gave him a perspective that no other place or time in his life would ever provide, and he was enthralled at the multitude of cultures he witnessed.[4]

Visitors could not help but notice, while traveling about the bustling seaport city, its strikingly high numbers of immigrants. The city flourished with African-descended, European, and Hispanic peoples from countries around the world. "No city perhaps on the globe," wrote visitor William Darby in 1817, "presents a greater contrast of national manners, language, and complexion, than does New Orleans."[5] Locals, too, extolled their city's cosmopolitan nature. "The population is much mixed," wrote John Adems Paxton in the 1822 city directory, "there is a great '*confusion of tongues*,' and on the Levée, during a busy day, can be seen people of every grade, colour, and condition: *in short it is a world in miniature*."[6]

A young and inexperienced Abraham Lincoln entered this polyglot world in 1828 and 1831. Virtually everywhere he looked, Lincoln would have been able to see examples of ethnic tension—in the streets, in conversation, and in the press. Local newspapers were filled with prejudice and scorn toward one group of immigrants or another. Editors of the local newspapers wrote inflammatory pieces foreshadowing the American, or Know Nothing, Party, which would rise in the 1850s to exploit American xenophobia. These editors gave their ironic assurance that their potential subscribers would be shackled by no particular party as they spewed forth their venom. Lincoln would have seen firsthand the difficult time some immigrants had in a city that was heavily populated by a foreign-born element. He was present in New Orleans when the Creoles in particular suffered at the hands of native-born Americans. After establishing alliances with the German and Irish immigrants, the Creoles quickly became an object of scorn. The presence, experience, and treatment of immigrant groups in New Orleans made an indelible impression on visitors like Lincoln. Later in his life he remembered what he saw as a youth and forcefully opposed the nativist movement of the 1850s and the Know Nothing Party, which was gaining popularity at the time.

It was also here that Lincoln saw the nation's largest concentration of free people of African ancestry, some of whom were extremely wealthy and well educated. While Lincoln never actually described the diversity he observed in New Orleans, he did edit William Dean Howells's writing on that topic in an 1860 campaign biography. After Howells marveled at "the many-negroed planter of the sugar-coast, and the patriarchal creole of Louisiana" without any edits by the candidate, Lincoln then made suggestions that resulted in a description of New Orleans as "that cosmopolitan port, where the French voyageur and the rude hunter that trapped the beaver on the Osage and the Missouri, met the polished old-world exile, and the tongues of France, Spain, and England made babel in the streets."[7]

A part of New Orleans even followed Lincoln to Springfield. William "Billy" Fleurville, a free black man of French-African ancestry, found New Orleans to be a hostile place to free people of color in the 1820s. Fearing kidnapping and enslavement, Fleurville fled New Orleans for St. Louis and then found his way up the Illinois and Sangamon Rivers in 1831. "While approaching the village of New Salem," a county history recorded, "he overtook a tall man wearing a red flannel shirt, and carrying an axe on his shoulder. They fell into conversation, and walked to a little grocery store together. The tall man was Abraham Lincoln, who soon learned that the stranger was a barber out of money. Mr. Lincoln took him to his boarding house, and told the people his business and situation. That opened the way for an evening's work among the boarders."[8]

Lincoln later persuaded Fleurville—who anglicized his name to Florville—to relocate in Springfield, where he married and raised a family, establishing a successful barbershop. Florville groomed Lincoln, who affectionately called him "Billy the Barber," through his attorney days, through the ups and downs of his forays into politics, and just before his final departure from Springfield to become president of the United States.

Over the years, it is likely that Lincoln enjoyed many conversations at Florville's barbershop on East Adams Street about New Orleans, immigrants, slavery, and the Mississippi River, with the bilingual, Catholic, French-African-Haitian-American man who became a friend. It would seem that their conversations were of substance, and certainly the foundations of a genuine friendship were there, as evidenced in a warm letter of gratitude that Florville wrote Lincoln after the Emancipation Proclamation went into effect earlier in 1863. "I thought it might not be improper for one so humble in life and occupation to address the President of the United States. Yet, I do so, feeling that if it is received by you . . . it will be read with pleasure as a communication from Billy the Barber." He continued, "I and my people feel gratitude to you for . . . your Proclamation. . . . The Shackels have fallen, and Bondsmen have become freemen to Some extent already. . . . And I hope ere long, it may be universal in all the Slave States. That your Authority May Soon extend over them all, to all the oppressed, releiving them from their Bondage, and cruel Masters; Who make them work, and fight against the Goverment. . . . May God grant you health, and Strength, and wisdom."[9] Lincoln's friendship with Florville may have been an influence when the president established official diplomatic relations with Haiti in 1862.

Interestingly, it was through Lincoln's connection with New Orleans and the efforts of several immigrants that the Great Emancipator freed his first person of color. While traveling in New Orleans in 1856, John Shelby, a free black man and son of one of Florville's fellow African American barbers in Springfield, found that same hostility directed toward him that Florville had experienced years earlier. Not having the proper papers to travel freely in the Crescent City, Shelby was arrested and imprisoned. Somehow, however, he made contact with a Springfield-raised New Orleans attorney named Benjamin Jonas and suggested that Jonas contact a prominent lawyer back home in Illinois whose influence might help his case and arrange for his release. Jonas recognized the name because Abraham Lincoln was a friend of his father, Abraham Jonas. Word of Shelby's arrest quickly reached his mother and then Lincoln. "Mr. Lincoln was very much moved," wrote one of Lincoln's early biographers, "and requested Mr. Herndon to go over to the State House, and inquire of Governor [William Henry] Bissell if there was not something that he could do to obtain the possession of the negro. Mr. Herndon made the inquiry and returned with the report that the Governor regretted to say that he had no legal or constitutional right to the [act]. Mr. Lincoln rose to his feet in great excitement, and exclaimed, 'By the Almighty, I'll have that negro back soon, or I'll have a twenty years' agitation in Illinois, until the Governor does have a legal and constitutional right to do something in the premises.'"[10]

Frustrated by the fact that the law was working against them, Lincoln and Herndon withdrew $60.30 from the Metropolitan Bank of New York and sent the funds to Benjamin Jonas's office in New Orleans on May 27, 1857. Jonas used the money to pay the fine and within a matter of a few short weeks secured Shelby's release and returned him to Springfield. Jonas warned Lincoln that if Shelby traveled south again, "be sure [he has] his papers with him—and he must also be careful to be away from the boat at night—without a pass [from] the captain."[11]

John Shelby thus became among the first, if not the actual first, African American ever freed by Abraham Lincoln. Shelby's New Orleans imprisonment surely would have resulted in his forced labor and quite possibly his permanent enslavement. Lincoln's affection for the Jonas family likely prompted him to take this action as much for them as for Shelby. Lincoln called Abraham Jonas "one of my most valued friends," and their friendship dated back to the 1830s.[12]

It is likely that the two Abrahams met and struck up a friendship shortly after Jonas arrived in Quincy, Illinois, in 1838. Both had already served their apprenticeship in politics: Lincoln for two terms in the Illinois state legislature and Jonas for four in the Kentucky House. It was natural that the two young politicians should gravitate toward each other, even though their backgrounds were so different.

Jonas had immigrated to Cincinnati, Ohio, from England in 1819 with a sizable group of Jews from Plymouth and Portsmouth, after his brother Joseph, the first Jew to settle west of the Allegheny Mountains, sent back news that life on the western frontier showed much promise. After several years in Kentucky, where he achieved success as merchant and politician, Jonas left for Illinois, a state that beckoned many other Kentuckians as well. One of the first Jewish settlers in the region, he lived first in Quincy and later moved to Springfield, where he became a prominent resident. In Illinois, he sought admission to the bar and political office on the Whig ticket, which naturally attracted him to Lincoln. Jonas became a strong supporter of Lincoln and remained so throughout the rest of Lincoln's life, actively campaigning for him in every election in which Lincoln ran. "Be assured," Jonas wrote Lincoln, "that nothing will afford greater pleasure to your personal friends and the Whigs generally than you consent to visit us—and the Douglasites would as soon see old nick here as yourself." When the old Whig Party finally died in the sectional strife over slavery, Jonas and Lincoln both decided to enlist in the ranks of the new Republican Party.

On several occasions, Jonas summoned Lincoln to Quincy to deliver one of his "sledge hammer speeches," at a meeting or on a stump on behalf of a local candidate. Jonas told Lincoln that his address would "effect wonders" and promised "the tallest kind of crowd" if his Springfield friend could arrange his schedule to make the trip. Lincoln trusted Jonas's political judgment and friendship, and he did not question when his friend needed him for personal or political reasons. For example, even though Lincoln was in the midst of his exhausting series of debates with Stephen Douglas, the political turning point of his life, Lincoln wrote back to Jonas, "My mind is at once made up to be with you."[13]

Once Lincoln entered the national stage, Jonas marched in lock-step with him. During the campaign, Jonas wrote Lincoln several confidential letters concerning the Democrats' attempts to draw the foreign-born vote away from Lincoln by painting him as an anti-immigrant Know Nothing Party member. Lincoln had denied the charge numerous times in the previous six years, but Jonas believed it was too dangerous to ignore. Ironically, the accusation centered around Lincoln's visit to Quincy back in 1854, a trip he had undertaken at Jonas's request and one in which he was hardly out of Jonas's sight long enough to attend any Know Nothing meeting that might have taken place. In a letter to Jonas, Lincoln recalled the details of his trip to Quincy and, without specifically saying so, suggested that Jonas was the logical man to make a public denial of the accusation. Lincoln was far too clever a politician to publicly repudiate the old Know Nothing voters at such a crucial time when every vote counted, but he had to protect the immigrant vote under all circumstances. While there is no record of Jonas's statements on the subject, it is entirely possible that he went to the Democrats and threatened to expose their attempt to misrepresent Lincoln's attitude toward the immigrants unless they called off their scheme. Whatever was Jonas's course of action, the Democrats never published any evidence of their charges.[14]

Shortly after Lincoln's election, Jonas sent the president-elect another confidential letter. He apologized for taking up valuable time, "when you have so much to think of and so many things to perplex you," but the matter was urgent. Jonas had many friends and relatives in the South, and he had just received a letter from New Orleans warning him of a plot by prominent Southerners to assassinate Lincoln before the inauguration. Jonas regarded the author of the letter as a cautious and reliable person who would not convey such information unless he was certain that it was authentic. Fearful for his friend, Jonas pleaded with Lincoln to take all precautions for his "personal safety and the preservation of our National Integrity." Jonas was certainly not among those who laughed and sneered a few months later when news leaked out that Lincoln had arrived in Washington under secret guard to avert a threatened attack on his train in Baltimore.[15]

Jonas was one not to ask for favors, but his friend Orville Browning knew that he hoped to be reappointed to the Quincy postmastership. Thus Browning wrote to Lincoln, "When the time arrives for appointing to offices throughout the country, I would be glad to have our mutual friend Abram [*sic*] Jonas remembered in connection with the Post Office at Quincy. He wishes the place, and, I think, ought to have it." Only a short time after the inauguration, Lincoln obliged his Quincy friend with the desired appointment.[16]

Other relatives of Abraham Jonas joined the Confederacy, including, paradoxically, the same Benjamin Jonas who had defended and obtained the release of John Shelby in 1857. Even in the midst of the terrible divisions caused by the war, President Lincoln remained friendly toward the entire Jonas family. As Benjamin later recalled, "Mr. Lincoln always asked after us when he saw any one from New Orleans during the war." When Abraham Jonas lay dying in Quincy, Illinois, Lincoln provided an emergency parole to Benjamin's imprisoned Confederate brother, Charles, so he could be with his father. It was none too soon, as Charles reached Quincy on the day of his father's death but, as he wrote with much gratitude, "in time to be recognized and welcomed by him."[17]

Two days after Abraham Jonas's death, Browning interceded again by asking Lincoln to appoint Jonas's widow to serve out her husband's unexpired term as Quincy postmaster. Lincoln did not hesitate to make the appointment and so paid one last tribute to his old friend, whose life had paralleled his own in many ways, who had shared many interests and principles with him, and who had been so loyal to him during all the disappointing years that had preceded his election to the highest office in the land.

Lincoln never forgot his experiences in New Orleans and as a flatboat operator, nor did he ever minimize the role in his personal development they had played. To a group of Sunday school students, Lincoln reminisced about his days on the river: "The only assurance of successful navigation . . . on the Mississippi," he explained, "depended upon the manner in which [the flatboat] was started. [And] so it is with you young folks. . . . Be sure you get started right as you begin life," he told them, "and you'll make a good voyage to a happy harbor."[18] Campaigning in 1843, Lincoln described his river experiences as having contributed significantly to his personal development. "It would astonish if not amuse, the older citizens of your County," wrote Lincoln, "who twelve years ago knew me a strange, friendless, uneducated, penniless boy, working on a flat boat—at ten dollars per month to learn that I have been put down here as the candidate of pride, wealth, and aristocratic family distinction."[19] Almost twenty years later, Lincoln returned to the same theme. "Free society is such that [a poor man] knows he can better his condition; he knows that there is no fixed condition of his labor, for his whole life. I am not ashamed to confess that twenty five years ago I was a hired laborer, mauling rails, at work on a flat-boat—just what might happen to any poor man's son!"[20]

Always the consummate politician, Lincoln took especial note of the foreign population in Illinois after his New Orleans adventures and as he commenced his political journey. Lincoln was a thirty-seven-year-old freshman member of the US Congress when the first Swedish settlement, the Bishop Hill colony, was created in Illinois. He had made the acquaintance of some of the Swedish immigrants during his days in the Black Hawk War, as several were named to the muster rolls of Captain Lincoln's company. And by the time Lincoln went to Washington, the Illinois prairies were studded with nearly two dozen Swedish communities. These horse-and-buggy towns were in large measure Lincoln's Illinois. Their establishment, growth, and development were coincidental with Lincoln's rise to prominence. The local newspapers that Lincoln read were exceptionally flattering of the Swedish immigrants. "A number of Swedes, about sixty or seventy, arrived by emigrant train," said the *Rock Island Weekly Republican*, adding, "They are a fine, healthy, neat looking crowd." The *Knoxville Republican* further complimented the Swedes in Lincoln's area: "They prove to be most valuable and exemplary citizens, sober, chaste, industrious, and intelligent."[21]

Lincoln, as a lawyer and later on his barnstorming political tours, frequently stopped at some of the Swedish settlements in his one-horse rig. Although he carried on no important legal business with the Swedes, he was aware of their activities, their farms, homes, newspapers, and business establishments. He saw them in the parades of the Wide Awakes, a paramilitary campaign organization affiliated with the Republican Party, and at political rallies. He mentioned them in his speeches, and he befriended several Swedish leaders who assisted him in his political campaigns.

Lincoln shared the sentiments of the Swedes in supporting the temperance movement that was growing in America. He had been an advocate for the movement while a member of the Illinois legislature, having introduced a petition "praying the repeal of all laws authorizing the retailing of intoxicating liquors." When asked if he belonged to the American Temperance Society, Lincoln replied, "I do not in theory, but I do in fact belong to the temperance society, in this, to wit, that I do not drink anything and have not done so for a very many years." This and his rail-splitting days endeared Lincoln to the Swedes. Many of the Swedes had swung an ax and many had lived in log huts, so Lincoln appealed to them as almost one of their own. They spoke of him as "*arbetaresonen* Lincoln," which translates to "Lincoln, the son of a working man." To the Swedes, Lincoln had lived the life of an immigrant. He was a man of the soil. He chopped his own wood, milked his own cow, fed his own horse, and cleaned his own stable. To J. L. Scripps of the *Chicago Tribune*, who had proposed to write a biography of him, Lincoln summed up his own life in terms the Swedes, if not all immigrants, could relate to: "It can all be condensed into a single sentence you will find in Gray's *Elegy*. 'The short and simple annals of the poor.' That's my life and that's all you or anyone else can make of it."[22]

The Swedes were delighted by Lincoln's fight against all measures that sought to limit the privilege of any class of citizens, especially those of the laborer and immigrant. "If a hired laborer worked as a true man, he saved means to buy land of his own, a shop of his own, and to increase his property. For a new beginner [the immigrant], this was the true, genuine principle of free labor," Lincoln told them. This was music to the Swedes' ears, and they credited the ease with which they could obtain land to "Lincoln's Homestead Law," which generally gave an applicant ownership, at no cost, of farmland called a "homestead," typically 160 acres of undeveloped federal land west of the Mississippi River.[23]

Although the first immigrant group Lincoln became politically and intimately aware of was the statistically dominant Germans, he could not overlook the Swedish population in his early rise to political prominence. He was aware of the activities of Swedish immigrants

Fredrika Bremer, Jenny Lind, and John Ericsson, who were receiving flattering publicity in the newspapers that Lincoln read. He noticed, too, the prospering Swedish settlements at Andover, Bishop Hill, Knoxville, Galesburg, and other Illinois communities, whose residents were potential voters for an aspiring candidate. On more than a few occasions, Lincoln mentioned "the Scandinavians among us" in his speeches, and he welcomed the support of their leaders.

The Swedes, in spite of their political inexperience, enthusiastically volunteered to participate in many of Lincoln's campaigns. They conducted political meetings and rallies on his behalf, founded newspapers, and organized clubs that campaigned vigorously for Lincoln and his political party. Led by political and religious leaders such as Hans Mattson, the Swedes marched with Lincoln over the years all the way to the White House. A Swedish newspaper from Galesburg called the *Hemlandet* published Lincoln's biography and portrait, describing him as a "'man of the people, from the people' whom all Swedes should follow." The *Svenska Republikanaran* of Galva, Illinois, and the *Frihetsvännen* of Galesburg vehemently defended Lincoln when his opposition criticized him or accused him of being anti-immigrant. "We shall fight the Democrats, Catholic, and Irish elements," the latter wrote in an editorial, "and [always] support Abraham Lincoln."[24]

Swedish support for Abraham Lincoln did not go unnoticed by the mainstream press. The *Chicago Press and Tribune* remarked that during one Lincoln rally, "a notable feature of the occasion and of the enthusiasm was the stand taken by our German and Scandinavian fellow citizens, the clubs of which were out in full force, headed by bands of music, with which at the close of the meeting, they paraded our principal streets." And later the same newspaper observed, "We must not fail to do justice to our German Republicans as well as their Scandinavian brethren for the zeal and energy with which they worked yesterday to put the finishing touches to the noble services they have rendered in the whole canvass."[25]

Given his support for the immigrant and workingman, it was not unusual at Lincoln rallies to see the Swedes waving banners that read *"Jemnlikhet utan afseende på födelseort"* ("Equality without regard to native place"). Throughout the political campaigns for Lincoln, the Swedes learned all about American bare-knuckle politics in the nineteenth century. One of Lincoln's Swedish friends, Carl Blomgren, recalled how the Swedes had to march to the polls in a body on election days to offset the votes of the Irish who had assembled the previous evening to vote early and often. A group of two hundred Swedes at Galesburg was promised work at Macomb, Illinois, but they became suspicious and refused to leave when they were instructed to bring their naturalization papers. They later learned that they were to be used to vote for the Democratic ticket, a ploy that appalled Lincoln when he learned of it.[26]

In one personal and little-known episode in Lincoln's life, he became friends with the Reverend Lars Paul Esbjörn, a Swede who was a professor at Illinois University. Lincoln's oldest son, Robert, attended Esbjörn's classes at this Lutheran school in Springfield, and Lincoln frequently called on the professor to discuss his son's studies, as the boy was not an enthusiastic student at the time. Lincoln even served on the school's board of directors. Esbjörn had political experience as a member of the city council of Princeton, Illinois. He was an outspoken opponent of "strong drink" and slavery, and Lincoln took a liking to him, since they shared similar political beliefs. Esbjörn became a loyal and consistent supporter of Lincoln, both in the press and on the stump, and his sons enlisted in the Union army, with one of them becoming the first Swedish soldier to fall in battle.

Lincoln remembered and rewarded the Swedes who had served him well during his political campaigns. He appointed O. E. Dreutzer American consul at Bergen, Norway, and G. J. Sundell became consul at Stettin, Germany, and later assistant to the consul general of Romania. Lincoln personally intervened in the promotion of C. J. Stohlbrand to brigadier general when no vacancy for that rank existed in his division. He accepted a company organized in New York that called itself the Naval Brigade, under the command of Gustaf Helleday. The men wished to serve on the gunboats of the coast defense. Lincoln insisted that they form an infantry unit, and the Union coast guard was established, with Helleday as its colonel. Lincoln also relied on the advice of some prominent Swedish leaders during his presidency: Count Piper, the Swedish resident minister; John Ericsson, inventor of the ironclad *Monitor*; and Admiral John A. Dahlgren, who designed many of the arms used by the Union forces all were called into Lincoln's confidence throughout the war. In the admiral's case, it became personal for Lincoln. "I like to see Dahlgren," Lincoln said. "The drive to the navy yard is one of my greatest pleasures. When I am depressed, I like to talk with Dahlgren. I learn something of the preparations for defense, and I get from him consolation and courage." On several occasions, including Thanksgiving 1864, Dahlgren recorded in his diary that he enjoyed his holiday meal, which he had privately with the Lincolns.[27]

Lincoln saw in the Swedes that which he saw in other immigrants: hardworking laborers who came to America to partake in the land of plenty. "I know the trials and woes of the workingmen [and immigrants]," he once told a delegation of strikers. "I have always felt for them." As such, Lincoln's attitude toward immigrants often manifested itself in the interests of the "laboring many." Consequently, he often eschewed the nativist leanings of the old Whig Party.

In 1844 Philadelphia was the scene of serious street fights between Irish and Catholic immigrants and anti-Catholic nativists. Churches were burned, hundreds of immigrant homes destroyed, and at least a score of people killed. For a brief time Philadelphia took on the appearance of a war-torn city, and the militia had to be called out to restore order. Public reaction to these events was swift and, indeed, led to a decline, albeit temporarily, in the growth of nativism. Out in Springfield Lincoln contributed his part to the condemnation of mob violence. On June 12 a group of prominent Whigs held a public meeting, at which Lincoln introduced motions deploring violence aimed at immigrants and denouncing the charge that the Whig Party was hostile to foreigners and Catholics.

The Democratic press could not help but report that "Mr. Lincoln expressed the kindest, and most benevolent feelings toward foreigners; they were [doubtless], the sincere and honest sentiments of *his heart*; but they were not of those of *his party*." The newspapers reported further that "Mr. Lincoln also alleged the Whigs were as much friends of foreigners as Democrats; but he failed to substantiate it in a manner satisfactory to the foreigners who heard him." At Lincoln's urging, however, the Whigs adopted his resolutions, which declared that "the guarantee of the rights of conscience, as found in our Constitution is most sacred and inviolable, and one that belongs no less to the Catholic than to the Protestant; and that all attempts to abridge or interfere with these rights, either Catholic or Protestant, directly or indirectly, have our decided disapprobation, and shall ever have our most effective opposition." The resolutions also stipulated that the immigrant should gain citizenship after "some reasonable test of his fidelity to our country and its institutions" and after dwelling "among us a reasonable time to become politically acquainted with the nature of those institutions."[28]

The Whigs and the Democrats were, of course, competing for the immigrant vote. But at the same time, both of them tried to attract and hold the support of the American-born. The dilemma became especially acute for Lincoln in the 1850s when, as a Free-Soiler and an incipient Republican, he faced the challenge of the rising American, or Know Nothing, Party, with its demand for limiting the political rights of the foreign-born in general and the Catholics in particular. He did not want to antagonize the Know Nothings, for he hoped to win them over to the cause of resisting the extension of slavery into the western territories. Yet he detested their prejudice and made his feelings known to everyone who inquired.

Like so many in the mid-nineteenth century, Lincoln's philosophy about immigrants was far more complicated than merely that which pertained to the free labor economy. Abraham Lincoln was a product of his times and his environment. And despite whatever economic advantages immigrants might represent, many men of his era saw every immigrant ethnic group, whether Irish, Jewish, German, or Swedish, as monolithic. On the other hand, Lincoln tended to perceive each individual and each group as distinctive. Because he saw the diversity of these groups, rather than simply lumping them all together as "foreigners" or "savages," Lincoln's relationships with individuals and groups of different ethnicities were as inconsistent as the man himself.

Lincoln's legendary tolerance and compassion notwithstanding, he uncritically accepted the dominant prejudices of the day on more than one occasion. As a politician, and not a reformer, who required the votes of other white people, he would have done well to conceal any doubts about the equality of any group if he ever held them. For example, accused by Stephen Douglas of advocating black equality, he issued his famous, if not infamous, quote in the Charleston, Illinois, debate in 1858: "I am not, nor have ever been, in favor of bringing about in any way the social and political equality of the white and black races. I am not nor have ever been in favor of making voters or jurors of negroes, nor of qualifying them to hold office, nor to intermarry with white people. And I will say in addition to this that there is a physical difference between the white and black races which I believe will forever forbid the two races living together on terms of social and political equality."[29] Lincoln never uttered similar words about any immigrant group. As white voting citizens, the immigrants whom Lincoln consistently courted seemingly represented no challenge to his racial beliefs but very valuable political capital to be gained.

During his one term as a congressman, Lincoln's public opposition to the US-Mexican War represented one of the few positions he publicly took on the government's policies toward Hispanics and Latin America. As a Whig member of the Illinois delegation to the US House of Representatives, he introduced in December 1847 a series of resolutions denouncing President James K. Polk's handling of the war. The following month, Lincoln delivered a meticulously argued speech in Congress exposing what he saw as the vagueness of jurisdiction along the Texas-Mexico border. Both countries, Lincoln felt, had a legitimate claim to ownership, thus rendering Polk's declaration of war unconstitutional and contrary to international law. Lincoln apparently had high hopes for this speech, but he was soon disappointed when the Democrats ignored his remarks and his fellow Whigs gave him only weak support. In principle, Lincoln did not oppose territorial expansion, as seen by his willingness as president to stimulate homesteading on western lands. Even the annexation of Texas had only partially offended his sensitivity about expanding slavery, because in that case Texas already existed as a slaveholding territory, and annexation did not entail the spreading of slave labor to new areas. Rather, Lincoln's opposition rested more on the fears that slavery might expand into Mexico, a free nation, and that Polk's handling of the crisis that precipitated the war represented a usurpation of war-making powers that the Constitution left exclusively to Congress. Lincoln wrote to his law partner, William Herndon, that Polk's actions placed the president where kings had always stood—one of the many allusions to the "divine right" theory that Lincoln would make. Arguing as the lawyer that he was, Lincoln's concern rested more with the legalities of the process by which land was acquired from Mexico than with the consequences of acquisition for the Mexican people.[30]

Like most westerners, Lincoln had a low opinion of Latin American civilization, and his references to Latinos were never flattering. In his debate with Stephen Douglas at Galesburg, Lincoln attacked the concept of popular sovereignty—Douglas's notion that the people of a territory should decide the slavery issue for themselves—by asking a hypothetical question as to whether Douglas would apply the doctrine in an acquisition like Mexico where the inhabitants were "nonwhite." "When we shall get Mexico," Lincoln asserted, "I don't know whether the Judge [Douglas] will be in favor of the Mexican people that we get with it settling that question for themselves and all others; because we know the Judge has a great horror for mongrels, and I understand that the people of Mexico are most decidedly a race of mongrels." Lincoln continued by explaining, "I understand that there is not more than one person there out of eight who is pure white, and I suppose from the Judge's previous declaration that when we get Mexico or any considerable portion of it, that he will be in favor of these mongrels settling the question, which would bring him somewhat into collision with his horror of an inferior race."[31]

Even if one makes allowance for the fact that these comments were uttered during an intense debate where serious race baiting was occurring, Lincoln also used derogatory comments about Hispanics in speeches where there was no apparent motive for him to do so. In describing the Cubans, he pulled no punches. "Their butchery was, as it seemed to me," Lincoln said in 1852, "most unnecessary and inhuman. They were fighting against one of the worst governments in the world [the Spanish]; but their fault was, that the real people of Cuba had not asked for their assistance; were neither desirous of, nor fit for, civil liberty." Later, in a patriotic speech extolling the innovation and brilliance of "Young America" as compared with the "Old Fogy" countries, crediting Americans' technological success to their intellectual powers of observation and experiment, Lincoln concluded, "But for the difference in *habit* of observation, why did Yankees, almost instantly, discover gold in California, which had been trodden upon, and over-looked by Indians and Mexican greasers, for centuries?"[32]

It was in this same speech that Lincoln made one of his few remarks about the peoples of Asia, the nonwhite group with whom he had the least acquaintance and about whom he had the least opportunity to think about. Although he had never been to Asia, and, for that matter, had barely been outside of the United States, Lincoln prejudicially claimed that intellectual curiosity and scientific progress were the exclusive domain of the Western world. He recognized Asia as the birthplace of "the human family" and concluded that Asians, like African Americans, were indeed human beings, but he described Asia as an ancient, crumbling civilization whose time had long since passed. "The human family originated, as is thought, somewhere in Asia," Lincoln said, "and have worked their way principally Westward. Just now, in civilization, and in the arts, the people of Asia are entirely behind those of Europe; those of the East of Europe behind those of the West of it; while we, here in America, *think* we discover, and invent, and improve, faster than any of them." Recognizing that perhaps he was on a bit of thin ice, Lincoln continued, "*They* may think this is arrogance; but they cannot deny that Russia has called on us to show her how to build steam-boats and railroads—while in older parts of Asia, they scarcely know that such things as S.Bs & RR.s exist. In anciently inhabited countries, the dust of ages—a real downright old-fogyism—seems to settle upon, and smother the intellect and energies of man. It is in this view that I have mentioned the discovery of America as an event greatly favoring and facilitating useful discoveries and inventions."[33] While neither respecting nor appreciating the cultures of Asia or Latin America, Lincoln, like many nineteenth-century nationalists, pandered to his audiences by emphasizing the attributes and virtues of the United States. At the expense of degrading other peoples, it was Lincoln's intention to convince his fellow countrymen that their nation would be next on "the great stage of history," a most successful strategy to flatter voters during his ascent into national prominence.[34]

Lincoln, generally speaking, was pessimistic about the possibility of white people accepting nonwhites as equals. Often he spoke in flattering praise of white Americans' technological and moral superiority while denigrating peoples of color, peoples with whom he had little actual contact. But Lincoln was a private person by nature and a political person by appearance. Thus how much of this represents the inner heart and mind of Lincoln may be a different matter.

Assuming, however, that his public record reflects his private sentiments, Lincoln believed the peoples of Asia and Latin America to be backward. In this regard, Lincoln surely may be considered an ethnocentric individual who measured other cultures and subcultures through the prism of his own and found them wanting; for him, what was right for white America was right for the world. The American system of constitutional government, and its accompanying economic progress, remained his most cherished ideals, ones that other nations and peoples should emulate if they could. And Lincoln knew that few politicians then had gained power by believing otherwise. Put simply, Lincoln constructed a worldview that accepted diversity, but in a condescending manner. Whereas he thought very little about the traditions and fates of nonwhites, he gave extensive consideration to the future of European Americans and European immigrants and their place in the United States. Paradoxically, Lincoln's understanding of whiteness would move him to embrace a broader interpretation of such concepts as equality, human rights, and natural rights than it would most of his contemporaries. In the end, his very concern for the institutions and freedom of the white race would lead him to a deeper appreciation for the rights of nonwhites.

Lincoln was witness to the literal transformation of America. During his lifetime, heightened immigration resulted in a diversity of population that even the founders could not have imagined. From 1846 to 1855, roughly Lincoln's formative years on a political stage, more than three million immigrants came to the United States, nearly half of them from Ireland alone and almost a million from Germany. With a foreign-born population of nearly four million by 1860, the nation's ethnic character had changed considerably from the Anglo-Saxon society, steeped in English traditions, that the founders had visualized. Prejudice against Irish and German immigrants assuredly continued, but the political reality was such that non-English immigrants ultimately would have to be accepted as voting citizens. In essence, Lincoln became politically mature as the meaning of whiteness changed to include certain immigrant groups such as the Germans, Irish, Scandinavians, and Jews.

The changes in Lincoln's hometown of Springfield were no different in many regards from those occurring in the United States at large. In his personal life and in his public addresses, Lincoln's awareness of these changes became manifest. His famous debates with Stephen Douglas came on the heels of the 1856 elections, in which the great mass of Irish immigrants voted for the first time. When Lincoln invoked the Declaration of Independence in those debates and later in his career, it was an expanded version that he framed within the country's growing diversity. Lincoln was acutely sensitive to the fact that many in his audiences were *not* part of that race of Anglo-Saxon Englishmen who had written the Declaration. He embraced that and welcomed them into his political fold.[35]

Politically pragmatic and personally compassionate, Lincoln understood full well that were the Declaration of Independence to be narrowly interpreted, then millions of immigrants, not to mention potential voters, would never become citizens of the United States. Lincoln attacked Douglas many times on his strict reading of the Declaration, as his opponent claimed that the founders had intended the document to apply only to themselves and fellow British subjects. The Declaration of Independence "has proved a stumbling block to tyrants," Lincoln asserted, "and ever will, unless brought into contempt by its pretended friends. Douglas says that no man can defend it except on the hypothesis that it only referred to British white subjects and that no other white men are included—that it does not speak alike to the down trodden of all nations—German, French, Spanish, etc., but simply that the English were born equal and endowed by their Creator with certain natural or equal rights among which are life, liberty and the pursuit of happiness, and that it meant nobody else. Are Jeffersonian Democrats willing to have the gem taken from the magna charta of human liberty in this shameful way? Or will they maintain that its declaration of equality of natural rights among all nations is correct?"[36]

Lincoln imagined that the Declaration was a set of ideas and principles that were meant to be inclusive of all peoples, not just people with English ancestry. To accept a less inclusive interpretation would mean the disfranchisement of recent immigrants who claimed equality within the white race. Interestingly and significantly enough, though Douglas never conceded that Lincoln was right, he nevertheless quietly dropped his use of "British subjects" when referring to the Declaration and replaced it with the words "white men" or "men of European birth."[37]

Despite its Anglo-Saxon origins, the Declaration of Independence, to Abraham Lincoln, by the mid-nineteenth century belonged to subsequent generations of European immigrants. The United States would thereby be opened to refugees from foreign lands. On some level, then, Lincoln foresaw the evolution of America from Anglo-American to Euro-American to its present multicultural state. Lincoln took great inspiration from immigrants and their ambition to move up in the world. He admired them and their drive to become proprietors of their own businesses, for Lincoln had been there himself. Only a country that allowed immigrants to fully partake in its bounty would be certain of success, he believed. And only seeing the Declaration of Independence as an invitation, rather than a rejection, could achieve that. "From the first appearance of man upon the earth, down to very recent times," Lincoln told an audience in Milwaukee, "the words 'stranger' and 'enemy' were quite or almost synonymous. Long after civilized nations had defined robbery and murder as high crimes, and had affixed severe punishments to them, when practiced among and upon their own people respectively, it was deemed no offence, but even meritorious, to rob, and murder, and enslave strangers, whether as nations or individuals. Even yet, this has not totally disappeared. The man of the highest moral cultivation, in spite of all which abstract principles can do, likes him whom he *does* know, much better than him whom he does *not* know. To correct the evils, great and small, which spring from want of sympathy, and from positive enmity, among *strangers*, as nations, or as individuals, is one of the highest functions of civilization."[38]

It remained to be seen whether the personal and the political Lincoln would reconcile with one another and demonstrate an enduring sympathy toward "strangers." And it also remained to be seen whether he could practice what he preached on a daily basis as he walked and rode the dusty streets of his growing Springfield and matured on his journey as a man, a lawyer, and a politician en route to the White House.

AWAKENING: COMING OF
AGE IN SPRINGFIELD

"Our short residence in Springfield," wrote the editor of the newly formed *Sangamo Journal*, "does not enable us to speak with certainty of the comparative improvement of the place in the last year with former years. We see enough, however, to convince us, that the advantages which Springfield offers to the merchant, the mechanic, and other professions, will not be much longer overlooked. Our population is rapidly increasing. A considerable number of buildings were erected last summer—many are now being built—and a still greater number are projected for the ensuing year." But Abraham Lincoln arrived in Springfield in 1837 alone, poor, with no relatives providing support, no friends waiting for him, and no connections to call upon. Depressed by his own poverty in a city that boasted fourteen hundred residents, eleven lawyers, eighteen doctors, and nineteen dry goods stores, Lincoln found Springfield to be worlds apart from his previous residence of New Salem and before that the uncultivated wilderness of Indiana from which he had departed to seek out educational and economic opportunities. Although Lincoln, perhaps more than any other individual, was responsible for putting Springfield on the map, the first few weeks in his new home were depressing ones. "This thing of living in Springfield is rather dull business after all," Lincoln concluded three weeks after his arrival. "At least it is to me. I am quite lonesome here as I ever was anywhere in my life. I have been spoken to by but one woman since I have been here, and should not have been by her if she could have avoided it. I've never been to church yet, and probably shall not be soon. I stay away because I am conscious I should not know how to behave myself."[1]

Although he never did become comfortable with the Springfield aristocracy, Lincoln was a keen observer of the human condition and soon became acutely aware of the people around him in and out of his new hometown. The road to Springfield took Lincoln through an area that for some time had been a virtual magnet for German immigrants, and he very likely noticed the growing importance of Germans relatively early in his life. As early as 1814 Germans had established settlements in Illinois on the Wabash River and in Brownsville in Jackson County. One contemporary described them as "industrious, though not enterprising people, usually farmers of moderate means, who lived comfortably, and kept their associations mainly among themselves."[2] By 1819 the wealthy German immigrant Ferdinand Ernst visited Illinois, and on learning that the small, muddy village of Vandalia on the Kaskaskia River was destined to become the state capital, he used his financial wherewithal to buy property and relocate almost ninety German families there.[3]

Fourteen years later Lincoln's legislative career began when he entered the Illinois State House of Representatives in Vandalia. By then Vandalia was a flourishing German settlement. It was here that Lincoln began the legislative journey that ultimately led to the White House. And part of Lincoln's skill was his cognizance of the political world in which he found himself. That awareness certainly included his recognition of the presence and importance of the German community around him.[4] Politically adroit as he was, Lincoln surely understood both the rural and urban value that German constituents in Illinois represented. Even though the census numbers indicated that by 1850 Germans constituted not quite 5 percent of the total population of Illinois, they nevertheless already made up 17 percent of the population of Chicago, Illinois' largest city.[5]

Indeed, the failure of the revolution of the German states from 1829 through 1849, especially the 1848 Revolution, resulted in the exodus of many middle-class Germans and skilled laborers to America. Such prominent men as Gustave Koerner, Friedrich Hecker, Peter

Joseph Osterhaus, Franz Sigel, Carl Schurz, and George Schneider all soon would be within the political orbit of Abraham Lincoln. The migration of German laborers and artisans became one of the fortuitous events in Lincoln's life, as they were a free labor-oriented body of industrious skilled workers who arrived in a growing city desperately in need of their labor. Too, they fit perfectly the economic philosophy that Lincoln espoused for most of his life, that of hardscrabble, working-class individuals who worked a hard day for an honest day's wage.[6] As the German and Irish populations grew in both rural and urban Illinois, it is difficult to imagine that Lincoln would not have taken them into any political considerations that he might have had.

Lincoln was no stranger to the city of Chicago. In the eleven years between July 5, 1847, when he first attended Chicago's River and Harbor Convention as a newly elected US congressman, and October 1858, after his famous debates with his political nemesis Stephen A. Douglas, Lincoln visited the city twenty times, frequently for extended visits. During this same period the number of immigrants here was rising, particularly the Germans on the North Side and Irish on the South Side. Lincoln also would have encountered German Jewish immigrants, whose numbers in the United States increased dramatically after the European Revolutions of 1848. Lincoln was keenly aware of the changes that the city was undergoing as its population changed. The architectural styles confirmed and accentuated the importance of Chicago's ethnic element, and Lincoln easily would have seen the presence and contributions of Germans and Irish to the city landscape. Ethnic church spires began to dominate the skyline, competing with grain elevators as the tallest structures in sight, and as he walked the streets of Chicago, Lincoln would have observed that some were named after prominent Germans, such as Goethe and Schiller on the North Side.[7]

The Germans also organized a number of secular clubs that ranged from mere social and singing organizations to political and secret societies such as the Masons and Odd Fellows, which factored significantly into Lincoln's political climb to the White House. Lincoln surely was aware of these clubs and, in all likelihood, interacted with them, because they so closely paralleled American political cultural expressions with their use of brass bands, oratory, singers, floats, uniforms, flags, fireworks, and gunfire.[8]

But it was in Springfield that Lincoln grew, matured, married, and developed his career. And not far from the brightly lit and tastefully decorated mansion of Ninian Edwards, Lincoln's future brother-in-law, lived numbers of people who spoke with heavy accents or in foreign tongues. Many were illiterate and had only recently escaped starvation and political oppression in foreign lands that were far removed from the prairie capital of Springfield. They helped build the mansions of the rich as skilled or, more likely, unskilled workers. They did the heavy lifting, dug the sewers, brushed the horses, and mopped the floors. They owned no property and little more than the clothes on their back.

Lincoln would have encountered these immigrants on a daily basis in Springfield, perhaps while traveling to his law office or to the capitol building. Few of the German immigrants in Springfield ever achieved the level of wealth that Lincoln's in-laws possessed, but they soon recognized their own importance in local politics, and once that occurred, they ceased to be an invisible minority.

Although he was a flourishing lawyer, Abraham Lincoln's political interests and ambitions could never be completely subordinated. Always an apt student of his state's voting patterns and election returns, Lincoln was well aware of the numerous pockets of German settlers who had fled to Illinois after their revolutions had failed in their homelands. Many of these Germans were talented intellectuals, and nearly all were antislavery in their sentiments. Lincoln found in them a constituency that he simply could not overlook. One of the Germans with whom Lincoln became acquainted was a "professor of languages" from Philadelphia, reported Dr. Amos Willard French, Lincoln's Springfield dentist. "We got up a class in German for him. I took German lessons with him," recalled French. "I don't remember anything we learned at the time. Lincoln told so many stories that we laughed at them instead of studying the lesson, I am afraid. No, I don't think he made a very apt scholar, though he probably learned as much as any of the rest of us."[9]

When it came to studying, however, Lincoln was a loner and always had been, but several personal reasons probably compelled him to attend these German lessons in an organized setting with a teacher. He perhaps felt a little sympathy for this unemployed professor, but he also must have thought that it was an especially good opportunity to further cement his relations with the German community in and around Springfield. Lincoln was associating more and more with Germans who had great potential to assist his political ambitions, and it would have greatly enhanced his standing within the German community if he could at least understand and speak a few words in their native tongue.

With this in mind, Lincoln corresponded with Friedrich Karl Franz Hecker, a German immigrant in exile residing on a farm in St. Clair County and the acknowledged leader of the German Republicans for the state of Illinois. After Hecker's home was destroyed in a fire allegedly set by opposition Democrats, Lincoln wrote, "We cannot dispense with your services in this contest [the presidential election of 1856] and we ought, in a pecuniary way, to give you some relief in the difficulty of having your house burnt. I have started a proposition for this, among our friends, with a prospect of some degree of success. It is fair and just; and I hope you will not decline to accept what we may be able to do."[10] Hecker and Lincoln had been named presidential electors at large for the Republican ticket in 1856. Both men campaigned that year for their party's standard-bearer, John C. Frémont, as well as candidates for state office. Although Frémont was unsuccessful in his bid for the presidency, and Lincoln lost in his attempt to become a vice presidential candidate, Republicans nevertheless swept all of the Illinois offices from the governor on down, with Germans contributing mightily to their victories.[11]

The *Weekly Advocate* of Belleville, Illinois, reported on October 18, 1856, that after his meeting with Hecker, Lincoln addressed a group and "referred to the Germans and the noble position taken by them in just and dignified terms. When he called down the blessings of the Almighty on their heads, a thrill of sympathy and pleasure ran through his whole audience. They all rejoiced that clap-traps, false issues and humbugs are powerless with the great heart of Germany in

America. *Lincoln* and *Hecker* were inscribed on many banners." The two men's paths crossed again later when Hecker became commander of first the 24th and then the 82nd Illinois Volunteer Infantry during the Civil War, in which Hecker fought gallantly and was seriously wounded at the Battle of Chancellorsville.

Lincoln never forgot his growing relationship with the German community. Regretting that he could not attend the Fourth of July celebration of the German Republicans of the Seventh Ward of Chicago in 1858, he wrote to Anton C. Hesing, the future mayor of Chicago and the acknowledged leader responsible for swinging his Chicago German constituents into the Republican Party, "I send you a sentiment: *Our German Fellow-Citizens*—Ever true to *Liberty*, the *Union*, and the *Constitution*—true to Liberty, not *selfishly*, but upon *principle*—not for special *classes* of men, but for *all* men; true to the Union and the constitution, as the best means to advance liberty."[12]

As his reputation became more widespread, Lincoln began to consider himself as a legitimate candidate for national office. Seeing the significance of the German vote in the recent election, Lincoln determined to purchase a German language newspaper, which he believed would further increase his standing with those immigrant voters. Dr. Theodore Canisius had come to the country in the 1850s from Prussia, where he had studied medicine. He settled first at Edwardsville, Illinois, and then at Alton, where he established the *Freie Presse* in 1858. Soon thereafter Canisius transferred his German language publication to Christian Schneider, who operated the press until 1859. After this sale Canisius moved to Springfield, where he edited another paper called simply the *Free Press*, an English translation of his former paper's name. The newspaper office that he opened was not far from Lincoln's law office.[13]

Lincoln made the acquaintance of this German physician who aspired to be a political journalist. Apparently, Canisius fell into debt and his printing press and type set was repossessed by another German, John M. Burkhardt, who planned to resell them. Seeing an opportunity for political gain, the politically astute Lincoln purchased the repossessed printing machinery for the Germans of Springfield. To accomplish this, he sought the aid of a friend, the banker Jacob

Bunn, to purchase everything for $400.[14] Thus on May 30, 1859, Lincoln signed a contract with Canisius, who would then publish a Republican newspaper in Springfield for him. It was "to be chiefly in the German language, with occasional translation into English at his option." The newspaper was to be published at least weekly. Canisius would be allowed to realize all profits, but he was to assume all expenses, and the political philosophy of the newspaper was to be consistent with the Republican Party of Illinois. The title of the new periodical was to be the *Illinois Staats-Anzeiger* (*Illinois State Advertiser*), and Lincoln agreed to furnish the printing press and type, which he would continue to own and control. The conditions set by Lincoln clearly show the importance he attached to reaching the German voter.[15]

Lincoln did write, however, that "if said Canisius shall issue a newspaper, in all things comfortable hereto, until after the Presidential election of 1860, then said press, types &c are to be his property absolutely, not, however, to be used against the Republican party; nor to be removed from Springfield without the consent of said Lincoln." Being associated with this German publication must have spurred Lincoln's interest in the German language, but he turned over the paper to Canisius on December 6, 1860, less than a month after being elected president. Lincoln recorded this transaction on the bottom of a piece of blue paper: "Dr. Theodore Canisius having faithfully published a newspaper according to the within, I now relinquish to him the press, types, etc., within mentioned, without any further claim of ownership on my part. A. Lincoln." The German paper had served its purpose well. Unfortunately, not a single issue exists today, and it is unknown whether the newspaper existed after 1860.[16]

Lincoln never forgot the loyal services of Dr. Canisius and appointed him as consul to Vienna in June 1861. Canisius served there for a number of years and even ultimately composed a German language biography of Lincoln, which he published in Europe. Additionally, after the Union defeat at Bull Run in July 1861, Canisius was asked to secretly offer a command in the Union army to the Italian military hero and politician Giuseppe Garibaldi. When this episode was discovered, it appeared that Canisius's diplomatic career in Italy was over. Nevertheless, he survived the controversy and the Italian government requested that he remain consul in Vienna, where he served until 1866.

Lincoln's relationship with the Germans had truly educated him in a culture that he could not have imagined as a young boy in Kentucky. Indeed, on his way to Washington, DC, to be inaugurated, he encountered Sigismund Kaufmann, a German Jew and another exile from the Revolutions of 1848. A brilliant lawyer and antislavery advocate, Kaufmann was taken aback when Lincoln conversed with him a little in the German's native language. "I know enough German to know that Kaufmann means merchant," said Lincoln, "and Schneider means tailor—am I not a good German scholar?" The former prairie lawyer joked that he had become almost bilingual.[17]

Lincoln's interest in the German vote transcended mere crass political expediency. At a time of rampant nativism, Lincoln sought to ensure that the Germans could cast their votes without fear of reprisals. And having known the value of native language newspapers himself, he wanted to provide the Germans with his speeches in their native tongue.

As Lincoln matured in his philosophy about free labor and free markets, and certainly in his opposition to slavery, he did not have to look very far to find visible evidence that his beliefs were not being practiced in regard to white laborers. For, along with the Germans in Springfield, the Irish constituted a visible immigrant population that occupied the lower ranks of the community of which Lincoln was part. Not far from his residence lived immigrant laborers whose experiences were confirmation that hardworking free laborers in Lincoln's own Springfield lacked opportunity and social mobility. "The white wage slave," decried the outspoken congressman Michael Walsh, "did not benefit from the fruits of his labor," but "after [he] has added by his labor and toil, wealth to the community in which he has lived, he is turned adrift without any, among all the different employers he has had, to give him a mouthful of victuals or a night's lodging."[18]

Still, the Irish had come to Illinois with hope and optimism. Congress in 1818 had authorized townships to be set aside in the state for emigrants fleeing Ireland's turmoil, with land sales at two dollars per acre. Hundreds of Irish emigrants had arrived in New York City in the spring of 1819, and many traveled inland to the prairies of Illinois. The lead mines in the Dubuque and Galena areas soon had Irish employees, and many counties recorded "Irish Settlement" by the late 1830s. The Irish, as well as other immigrant groups in Illinois, lived on hope: hope for rich harvests from the prairie soil; hope for the new towns already growing and for those only in the minds of the speculators; hope for the prosperity promised by roads, canals, railroads; and hope for the West, which was increasingly hailed as the nation's future center of political and economic power.

Springfield, however, became a dream deferred for many of the Irish immigrants. As Catholics, the Irish found that hostility existed toward them from their arrival. "Intemperance, Sabbath-breaking, and profanity from all around us, from the very outset of settlement," complained one preacher. "If the gospel of Christ be not there," the Springfield Presbyterians and Congregationalists were told, "Romanism will be there, or Mormonism, or Millerism, or Mesmerism, or Spiritual Knockings, or some other equally stupid and debasing form of faith or infidelity." Irish immigrant leader Thomas D'Arcy McGee sent a warning to Catholic leaders back in Ireland: "There is now going on here a hand-to-hand battle for Faith, unprecedented, I verily believe, since the 'Reformation,' in any quarter of the world."[19]

While the Germans felt antagonism toward the South and slavery, an attitude that was more in tune with Lincoln's, most of the Irish in Springfield were not moved by the abolitionists' arguments. Perhaps this difference can best be explained by their contrasting European backgrounds. Blocked in their attempts to obtain land in the German states, the Germans of Springfield, like their brethren elsewhere in the United States, saw their dreams coming true in America until the specter of a slave-owning West was suddenly spread before them in the 1850s. The Irish came from a different environment, one that included conflict with Protestant proselytizers and British officials, many of whom were critics of slavery as well as Catholicism. "In some cases," commented an Irish clergyman, "the agitator for abolition was also an agitator against the Catholic." Since Britain was constantly presented as the world's antislavery leader, many of the

Irish in Springfield found it difficult to adopt the philosophy of their traditional enemy.

Lincoln was well aware of the attitude of Springfield's Irish toward slavery. The anti-Catholic *Chicago Tribune*, which Lincoln read regularly, presented the popular notion that the Irish supported slavery out of fear that freed blacks would replace them in the labor market. Without slavery, the *Tribune* asserted, there would be no class of people beneath the Irish in Illinois in particular and America in general.

Many of the Irish immigrants in Springfield may well have felt left out of America's success story and agreed with the words of Michael Walsh. They filled the bottom of the occupational ladder and often had little or no property to show for their labor. Abraham Lincoln, on the other hand, was one of Springfield's most prominent citizens, and he was a living symbol of the success of the free labor social ladder. He would have had daily exposure to the deficiencies of the wage-earning system that he supported so strenuously on his simple journeys in and around the town that he loved so much. This exposure surely would have deepened his commitment to a labor system in which a man's daily wage was commensurate with his daily labor.

For Lincoln, the German immigrants in Springfield were loyal political supporters, and he knew that and cultivated them. The Irish, however, posed fundamental problems to Lincoln and his political aspirations. The Irish were steadfastly loyal to the Democratic Party and were already learning in Springfield how to master the American political system. Lincoln, like many former Whig politicians, blamed political defeat on the Democrats "colonizing" the Irish vote. Before Election Day in his 1858 senatorial campaign against Stephen Douglas, Lincoln remarked, "I now have a high degree of confidence that we shall succeed, if we are not over-run with fraudulent [Irish] votes to a greater extent than usual." Lincoln lamented that he had seen "Celtic gentlemen, with their black carpet-sacks in their hand," in several of the closely contested voting districts and that they were suspiciously loitering "about the doggeries." "I was told about four hundred of [Irish who] were brought into Schuyler, before the election, to work on some new railroad," Lincoln said, "but on reaching here I find that . . . is not so." Candidate Lincoln worried that the

Irish would lie about their residence and vote fraudulently in areas where he could ill avoid additional opposition, even though citizen Lincoln was well aware of the Irish plight just a short distance away from his home. "What I dread," Lincoln wrote, "is that they will introduce into the doubtful districts numbers of men who are legal voters in all respects except *residence* and who will swear to residence and thus put it beyond our power to exclude them."

Lincoln was so unnerved he suggested, "When there is a known body of these voters, could not a true man, of the '*detective class*,' be introduced among them in disguise, who could in the nick of time, control their votes? . . . It would be a great thing, when this trick is attempted upon us, to have the saddle come upon the other horse." Lincoln believed that this Irish constituency was part of the "float-ing Hibernian" population selling their votes to the Democrats. His law partner, William Herndon, assured Lincoln that the rumor of imported Irishmen was "no humbug cry," and Herndon reinforced that sentiment to a Massachusetts correspondent when he asked, "What shall we do? Shall we tamely submit to the Irish, or shall we arise and cut their throats? If blood is shed in [Illinois] to maintain the purity of the ballot box, and the rights of the popular will, do not be at all surprised."[20]

These comments show not only that Lincoln was more than ready to play hardball when it came to political campaigns, but also, perhaps more significantly, that Lincoln, like many other former Whig politi-cians, accepted the common stereotypes of Irish voters as being pawns of the Democratic Party bosses. Too, although he saw firsthand the poverty that characterized the Irish neighborhoods in his hometown and elsewhere, Lincoln blithely accepted the notion that the Irish were so poor that they carried their belongings in shabby carpetbags while spending what little money they had in the local saloons.[21]

Shortly thereafter, the *Jacksonville Sentinel* took Lincoln to task for his seemingly anti-Irish attitude by accusing him of entertaining "a holy horror of all Irishmen and other adopted citizens who have suf-ficient self-respect to believe themselves superior to the negro. What right have adopted citizens to vote Mr. Lincoln and his negro equality doctrines down? He would doubtless disfranchise every one of them if he had the power. His reference to the danger of his being voted down by foreigners, was a cue to his followers, similar in character to the intimation of the Chicago Press a few days since, that the republicans of the interior counties should protect their rights; in other words, that under the pretext of protecting their rights, they should keep adopted citizens from the polls. . . . every adopted citizen, be a democrat or republican, should have his vote. And every foreigner . . . who is a legal voter, *will have his vote* in spite of Mr. Lincoln."[22]

Such was obviously not the case, but it was indeed true that Lincoln's political acumen enabled him to separate his civic sympathies for the Irish plight from his drive for elected office. So serious, in fact, was Lincoln in his desire to ensure that the Irish prevented no one from casting their votes in elections, be they votes for him or for others, that he actually intervened to prevent possible voter intimidation. Herndon later recalled, "Once in Springfield, the Irish voters meditated taking possession of the polls. News came down the street that they would permit nobody to vote but those of their own party. Mr. Lincoln seized an axe-handle from a hardware store and went alone to open the way to the ballot-box. His appearance intimidated them and we had neither threats nor collisions all that day."[23] The former rail-splitter was still willing to use the tools of his former trade to protect the rights that he held sacred.

In many ways, though, what Lincoln saw in his hometown was a snapshot of America. The city's population doubled during Lincoln's time there, and with the changes in demography, the character of Springfield, as in much of America, was also rapidly and constantly changing. The 1850s witnessed the greatest rate of foreign immigration in the nation's history, bringing the first great wave of non-English and non-Protestant immigrants to America. At the beginning of the decade, immigrants constituted about a third of Springfield's population, but the proportion increased to 50 percent by decade's end. The Irish and Germans, in particular, doubled in their representation in the city. This was not insignificant to Lincoln, for at the time of his election to the presidency, 20 percent of Springfield's population was Irish and almost the same percentage was German. While the German and Irish populations more than doubled, the number of Springfielders from Kentucky rose by only nine individuals during the decade, less than one per year. The city's booming economy also exaggerated the chasm between rich and poor. By 1860, 10 percent of Springfield's men were unemployed, and the wealthiest 25 percent owned 97 percent of all the property in the city. Immigrants crowded into a squalid block of buildings on the north side of the public square known as "Chicken Row," because many of them survived by raising chickens and selling them to the city's middle-class housewives.[24]

Not far from Lincoln's home, the poverty of the immigrant community bred crime, and a "dangerous class" emerged to threaten the peaceful world of the upper class. A new variety of criminals emerged to replace the traditional horse thieves and gamblers of an earlier generation. Burglars, "house thieves," pickpockets, vandals, street fighters, and confidence men all occupied their places within the Dickensian urban environment. "Mud holes in our streets, doggeries in full blast every day in the week, more specially on Sundays, when we have also the firing of guns, general rows, and street fights," complained the *Springfield Illinois Journal*, "these are the comforts of the day." The local newspaper went on to enumerate other ills of the community, saying that "broken pavements, broken windows, broken fences, screeching and howling of drunkards, these are the comforts of the night." Certain ethnic neighborhoods were labeled "Battle Row" by the native Springfielders.[25]

Lincoln's neighbors blamed a good deal of the troubles on the immigrants. Local newspapers began "Police News" columns, which never failed to list the nationality of the criminals involved. The newspaper stories that Lincoln read at home and at his law office sounded like an indictment of immigration: a German immigrant was cut with a knife at a beer house, Irish railroad workers brawled in the Old Town, and a Frenchman killed an Irishman over a five-dollar debt. The "fall fighting season," cautioned the newspapers, was sure to erupt near election time. And so it did. As local elections approached, so too did the antipathy among the various immigrant groups as politicians promised panaceas to their problems and demonstrative appreciation for their support.

Yet Lincoln seemed somewhat oblivious to the pejorative stereotypes that the press was promulgating about various immigrant groups. As newlyweds Abraham and Mary Lincoln did not have much money and lived in rental properties for well over a year after they were married. During that time Mary took on the sole responsibility for care of their home, while Abe worked to establish his law career. In 1844 they were able to purchase a small home at Eighth and Jackson Streets, and they were later able to arrange for hired help to assist with the extensive work that accompanied maintaining a home and caring for a family, including a baby son. Most middle-class families had hired help, and for the Lincolns the assistance was especially needed during the next seventeen years, which saw the birth of three more sons, the expansion of the home to double its size, and the rise of Lincoln from successful attorney to president-elect. The Lincolns employed help that reflected the population of Springfield, including recent immigrants from Portugal and Ireland, as well as African Americans and white employees who had lived in the United States for many years.

The hired women ranged in age from eighteen to seventy-five years old. Most were single or widowed. The average wage was between $1 and $1.50 per week. Depending on the individual's situation, a portion of her pay went toward room and board. The general jobs performed by these women could include laundress, cook, governess or child-care provider, seamstress, and server. Other duties were more menial, including making fires, emptying chamber pots, cleaning lamps, and carrying water from the well and cistern.

Some of the people within Lincoln's employ lived with the Lincoln family. When the 1850 census was taken, Catherine Gordon, an eighteen-year-old woman from Ireland, was listed as a resident. Ten years later, the census revealed that Mary Johnson, a woman of Irish descent, resided at the Lincoln home. Other hired help that worked for the Lincolns did their work and returned home to their own families. Lincoln's neighborhood, and Springfield in general, reflected the growing diversity of peoples migrating to the area, and Lincoln accepted this reality without pause or resistance.

Indeed, Abraham Lincoln was present in November 1849 when 130 immigrants arrived in Springfield from Madeira, Portugal, to escape religious persecution. This group of exiles quickly established a new church called the Second Portuguese Presbyterian Church, and they eagerly made Springfield their new home. As part of this group, Charlotte Rodrigues was six years old when she arrived in Springfield with her father, Joseph, in 1849. Eleven years later she became a seamstress for Mary Lincoln. She labored eleven hours a day working on dresses that Mary wore while entertaining guests during Lincoln's candidacy and while he was president-elect.[26] Another member of the group, Frances Affonsa, was a "black eyed Portuguese woman" who did the family laundry for the Lincolns and stayed on to become the regular cook. The Lincolns very much liked Frances's cooking, and apparently she even managed to please Mary, who had already established quite a reputation among the domestic help as someone very difficult to satisfy.[27]

Lincoln became quite familiar with his Portuguese neighbors and accepted them readily in both a social and professional sense. When the Portuguese arrived in Illinois, Lincoln had just completed his sole term as a US congressman and returned to Springfield to open his law office with William Herndon. In the next dozen or so years, Lincoln crossed paths with the newly arrived Portuguese residents many times in various circumstances. He developed a very warm relationship with Antonio Mendonsa, whose family sold fresh fruit and vegetables to Springfield's elite. The older man could not speak English and took his young son John along with him to interpret. Lincoln "would invariably walk up to father, shake his hand most cordially, and utter some little pleasantry which I would interpret," recalled John many years later. "This interpretation seemed to amuse him very much. In every way he was most considerate. If the day was hot, the maid was instructed to prepare cooling refreshments of some sort, and *vice versa*. Knowing our reduced circumstances, he would take me by the hand, after father had been paid, and place a quarter therein, saying 'Sonny, take this to your mother to buy meat for dinner.'"

Quite in character, Mary always haggled with Mendonsa over the price of his goods, but the few times Lincoln was present, he tended to pay full price. Mendonsa's son John recalled such an incident: "We hunted for blackberries all morning, for at that time they were getting scarce. We were gone until 11:30 in the forenoon, and all father got was 3 pints. He took them to Mrs. Lincoln, but when she saw them she complained because they were so small. Father told me to tell Mrs. Lincoln these were the last picking; they were smaller than the last, but no more were to be found. . . . Mrs. Lincoln wanted to know what father asked for these. Father thought they should be worth fifteen cents a quart, considering the scarcity of the berries and the length of time consumed—from four A.M. until eleven. Mrs. Lincoln thought this price outrageously high, and said she would not pay more than ten cents. Father said he could not afford to sell for that and had me explain to her our long walk through the heat, but she was inexorable. We met Mr. Lincoln at the gate as we were leaving. He greeted father and asked me why we did not sell the berries to Mrs. Lincoln. I told him that we only had 3 pints . . . and that Mrs. Lincoln wanted to give father only 10 cents for them. He patted me on the head, smilingly and said, 'Sonny, you tell your father we'll take them.' . . . He paid father twenty-five cents and brother-in-law thirty cents. Mr. Lincoln quietly said, 'Mary they have earned all they ask for them. Get me a pan in which to put them.' She refused, saying 'No, I won't! I won't have them! I don't want them!' He then called to the maid. She brought a pan. . . . He chatted [with us] a while, and as he bade us good-by, gave me a quarter, telling me to be a good boy." Although it is a simple story, this episode poignantly demonstrates the kindness and consideration Lincoln showed toward immigrants and their labor, which underscored much of the political and economic philosophy that he espoused throughout his life.

Lincoln became so impressed with Mendonsa's work ethic that he hired him to do chores around his home. "My father," John wrote, "used to work for Mr. Lincoln, tending his garden and sawing wood. . . . At the time Mr. Lincoln had his office on the northwest corner of the square over the Stebbins' hardware store. I often went to the office with father to get the pay for the work done. . . . I hardly ever went there that Mr. Lincoln did not make me a present of a piece of money and pat me on the face and say: 'Now, you be a good boy. Come again.'"

John spoke warmly and glowingly about his family's relationship with Lincoln. "Mr. Lincoln was a great friend to the poor man and a great lover of little children. The last time I saw him, father and I, was after his election. It was that sad morning at the old Great Western Depot, when he bid all farewell from the rear platform of the last car. He saw father standing by, and reached his hand down and shook father by the hand and bade him goodby. It was the last time we saw him alive."[28]

Lincoln's support for the Portuguese community in Springfield transcended their hiring and the purchase of their goods. As Lincoln's law practice flourished, he frequently found that he had a little extra money to spend. In many instances Lincoln sought to invest his money where he thought it would bring a good return. One of the best investments of the day was in making small loans. These loans, which were generally made to individuals for a short term, frequently paid an interest of up to 20 percent.

The records indicate that in the 1850s Abraham Lincoln made seventeen such loans. Fifteen of these were made to men. The remaining two loans were made to a woman who is described in the record as "a Portuguese woman." Among the exiles from Madeira was Ritta Angelica da Silva, who owned a parcel of land not far from Lincoln's law office. It was in this general area that most of the Portuguese in Springfield had settled. On August 11, 1854, Lincoln made a loan of $125 at 10 percent interest payable annually. Ritta signed the promissory note with the understanding that the principal would be paid in four years. To secure the loan, Lincoln accepted a first mortgage on the parcel of land owned by da Silva.

Ritta paid the interest promptly but could not reduce the principal. In fact, eighteen months after receiving the first loan, she applied to Lincoln for a second loan of $125, which the lawyer granted. The terms were the same, 10 percent interest payable annually, with the loan to be paid in four years. Lincoln's interest rates were not exorbitant. At simple interest they were at a rate lower than that charged by banks for small loans then and for a long time thereafter. Lincoln made his loan to da Silva at some personal risk, for the land was probably not worth more than the amount granted, and he might well have failed to receive just return if he had decided to foreclose.[29]

Ritta, however, paid the loans in full, for the record shows that on November 26, 1858, shortly after Lincoln's defeat for the US Senate, the first loan was paid and the mortgage released. Lincoln deposited the money into his bank on the same day. On June 9, 1860, three weeks after Abraham Lincoln was nominated for president, the second loan was repaid and the second mortgage released. Lincoln's faith in the Portuguese woman was vindicated, and he found that his support of the Portuguese community in particular, and immigrants in general, would pay political dividends for him in November.[30]

Through his connection to the Portuguese whom he had met, Lincoln became aware of the problems and issues facing them. By 1855 almost four hundred Portuguese were living in Springfield not far from Lincoln, and they continued to arrive from Trinidad and Madeira. Certainly in their first generation in Springfield the Portuguese socially sought to maintain their ethnic culture. They formed three Portuguese Presbyterian churches in Jacksonville, Illinois, and two more in Springfield. Lincoln's awareness of the local churches came through some of his clients at the Lincoln and Herndon law firm, but his more personal interest stemmed from his family's employment of Frances Affonsa.

Affonsa's conscientious work favorably impressed the Lincolns. As laundress, Frances was junior in the household to Mariah Vance, a pipe-smoking black woman ten years older than Abraham Lincoln, who had served the Lincoln family since 1850. Mariah's son Billie became a close friend of Lincoln's oldest son, Robert Todd, who taught him to read and write. Although her veracity has been questioned in recent years, Mariah's observations of the Lincoln household recounted that Lincoln took such an interest in Frances's church that when the Second Portuguese Presbyterian Church found itself short on funds, he made several financial contributions to it before and after he was nominated for president. Lincoln's charitable and kindly contributions apparently encouraged others in the Springfield community to help out as well.[31]

Lincoln's years in Springfield not only prepared him for the political path on which he embarked but also significantly exposed him to immigrants and their cultures. For example, during his years in Springfield and when he rode the Eighth Judicial Circuit, Lincoln patronized Jewish businesses and socialized with members of Springfield's Jewish community. A young immigrant peddler from Cincinnati named Samuel Huttenbauer said that he often sold Lincoln suspenders and collar buttons, and that the future president always had a kind word and a story to tell to him. Lincoln also frequented Julius Hammerslough's haberdashery, and the two men maintained a cordial friendship, often discussing the challenges of clothing a six-foot, four-inch lanky body. In other Illinois towns outside of Springfield, Lincoln shopped at Henry Rice's general store when he visited Jacksonville and always lodged in the front section of Louis Salzenstein's clothing store when in Athens. As with his interactions with other immigrant groups, Lincoln learned from, and sympathized with, the Jewish immigrants he encountered during his legal career. These memories would remain with Lincoln for the rest of his life.[32]

While Lincoln was prospering as a lawyer and growing in reputation as a leader and politician, so too did Springfield grow. The once small prairie town was booming, as were so many cities in the old northwest, and their populations were increasing not only in number but in diversity as well. While slavery, its expansion, and its very existence were commanding the nation's attention and the politicians' rhetoric, the foreign-born element in America was coming of age politically. Merely by traveling to work, Abraham Lincoln was reminded of the immigrant population and their plight in their new homeland. And he remained committed to the principles that he had established as a young man in regard to free labor and a man's right to his wage earned. He practiced what he preached when it came to employing immigrants in and around his household, and his attitude toward the foreign-born was not unlike that which he held toward the slaves in the South. To Lincoln, all were entitled to their natural rights and compensation for the work they accomplished.

Perhaps what Lincoln was not prepared for was the ill winds of nativism that would soon blow across the land. A third political party would soon grow to be a political force to be reckoned with. The American Party, or the Know Nothings, as they were more popularly known, would attempt to overshadow the major parties and insinuate their anti-immigrant attitude into the American mindset. Though they were dismissed by some as nothing more than bigoted zealots who failed to understand the major issues of the day, the Know Nothings would almost immediately achieve a virtual meteoric success and, by so doing, force all major political figures to either accept or confront them. By no means was Abraham Lincoln immune to this, and consequently his political future and that of his fledgling Republican Party would soon be at stake. Lincoln was about to walk a very narrow political tightrope as the bonds of Union loosened all around him.

The second-oldest image of Lincoln was taken in 1854 at George Schneider's request by Johan Carl Frederic Polycarpus von Schneidau at his studio next door to Schneider's antislavery newspaper, *Illinois Staats-Zeitung*. Both Germans recognized that Lincoln was a valuable ally in the fight against the Kansas-Nebraska Act. Lincoln was holding Schneider's vehemently antislavery newspaper in the original photo, which was lost. When it resurfaced in 1858, Lincoln was holding the *Chicago Press and Tribune*, as seen here. Abraham Lincoln Presidential Library and Museum.

George Schneider (1823–1905) was an Illinois journalist and banker who, as one of the original Forty-Eighters, had fled his German homeland in the wake of revolution. His antislavery newspaper, *Illinois Staats-Zeitung*, provided valuable support to Lincoln in his political campaigns. Schneider was a delegate to the 1860 Republican National Convention, and Lincoln rewarded him for his loyalty by appointing him consul at Elsinore, Denmark. Abraham Lincoln Presidential Library and Museum.

Gustave Koerner (1809–96) was an Illinois lawyer, politician, and historian. He emigrated from Germany in 1833, was elected to the Illinois House of Representatives in 1842, served on the Illinois Supreme Court in 1845–48, and was lieutenant governor of the state in 1853–57. A staunch supporter of Lincoln, Koerner raised troops from Illinois for the Northern war effort and was assigned as an aide to General John C. Frémont before being appointed US ambassador to Spain. Abraham Lincoln Presidential Library and Museum.

Carl Schurz (1829–1906) was a German revolutionary, accomplished journalist, editor, orator, and statesman. One of the Forty-Eighters, he immigrated to Philadelphia and then moved to Wisconsin, where he joined the Republican Party and became a strong supporter of Lincoln. Lincoln appointed him US ambassador to Spain before making him a brigadier general in the Civil War, in which he served with his German regiments. After the war, he had a successful political career as a US senator and later secretary of the interior. Abraham Lincoln Presidential Library and Museum.

Dr. Theodore Canisius (1825–85) studied medicine in his German homeland before immigrating to the United States and establishing a newspaper in Alton, Illinois. After moving to Springfield, where he published the *Illinois Staats-Anzeiger*, he met Lincoln and the two became friends. Lincoln later rewarded Canisius for his loyalty with diplomatic posts at Vienna; Geestemunde, Germany; Bristol, England; and the Samoan Islands. Courtesy of the Library of Congress.

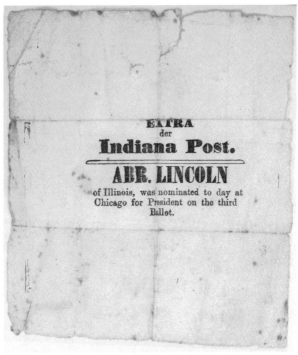

The *Indiana Post* was a Lafayette paper in German during the time of the 1860 presidential campaign and probably a bit longer. No known copies of the full newspaper have survived. Most likely, it was four pages a week. This handbill was found in an eastern Illinois house in 2012. It provided news of May 18, 1860, when Lincoln was nominated in the "Wigwam" at the National Republican Convention in Chicago. Obviously, some of the *Post*'s readers were English readers, too, as this example is an unusual piece of half-assimilated newsprint. Abraham Lincoln Presidential Library and Museum.

Isachar Zacharie (1827–1900) was an English-born Jew who trained in chiropody and called himself a doctor, though he never attended college or medical school. He immigrated to the United States in the mid-1840s and worked in several cities before settling in Washington, DC, in 1862. Zacharie's reputation for treating foot pain attracted Edwin Stanton, William Seward, and eventually Lincoln himself. Lincoln and Zacharie soon became friends, and the president sought his advice on many matters, especially regarding Jewish affairs. Lincoln so trusted Zacharie that he sent him into the South on several information-gathering missions. American Jewish Historical Society, New York City, New York, and Newton Centre, Massachusetts.

Major General Franz Sigel (1824–1902) was German-born and military trained. He immigrated to the United States as one of the Forty-Eighters, teaching in New York City public schools and becoming the director of St. Louis public schools on the eve of the Civil War. When war broke out, Sigel was commissioned as a colonel in the 3rd Missouri Infantry and recruited and organized German immigrants into the Union army. Looking for the support of antislavery, pro-Unionist immigrants, Lincoln took notice of Sigel's popularity with the Germans and promoted him to brigadier general in 1861, one of the president's early appointments of "political generals." Despite a controversial military career, Sigel eventually was promoted to major general. Abraham Lincoln Presidential Library and Museum.

ENLIGHTENMENT: KEEPING AFLOAT
IN THE ERA OF KNOW NOTHINGS

With great deliberation Senator Henry Wilson of Massachusetts rose on the Senate floor to rail against immigrants.
"The American [Know Nothing] movement proposes to correct these
evils and abuses by wise and humane legislation," he declared. "To
protect ourselves from the organized system in the Old World, which
subjects us to the support of foreign paupers and the depredations of
alien criminals; to thoroughly revise the naturalization laws."[1] Wilson was not alone in his beliefs. Political animosity toward foreigners
reached a zenith in the mid-1850s with the formation of the powerful
and fast-growing Know Nothing Party, which became a major con-
tender with Lincoln's new Republican Party for votes. The nativist
Know Nothings, the name of which implied that members were not
to divulge any of the society's secrets, led a popular crusade against
immigrants across the country, and Lincoln's Springfield neighbors
were not immune to their sentiments. When slavery emerged as
the critical issue in America, it was difficult to continue to label
the immigrants as the enemy, especially when large numbers of immigrants, especially the Germans, were joining in the antislavery
campaigns. But the Know Nothings were able to do just that. This
nativist party thrived on the broadly based anti-Catholicism of the
era and benefited from the anti-immigrant feelings generated by
fears of foreign labor competition, as well as the growing temperance reform movement.

With this sort of linkage to reformers, the Know Nothing party spread rapidly across the Midwest and Lincoln's Illinois. "There was scarcely a day but fist fights and rows between Know-Nothing rowdies and German and Irish born citizens took place," wrote a German newspaper editor. Know Nothing lodges and newspapers were in operation by 1854 in many Illinois cities and towns, including Springfield. According to a friend of Stephen Douglas, there were at least seventeen Know Nothing lodges in the Quincy area alone. "The smallest number of Democrats in any of them is twenty," he said, "which makes the changes enough to upset our majority and lose the district." Usually running as the American Party, the Know Nothings required party members to be Protestant born, reared, and wed, and to swear to vote only for native-born American citizens, excluding all foreigners and aliens "and Roman Catholics in particular." The mere thought of the Know Nothing presence was recorded in the Illinois press. The *Chicago Literary Budget* reported tongue in cheek, "Some folks think pretty loud that there is a body of men somewhere around who are rather more than sum [*sic*] pumpkins. . . . The name of Know Nothing is attached to them but nobody knows anything about such an organization. Travel from Dan to Beersheba and no such men can be found, but that there is something and somebody, somewhere and sometime, is quite certain."[2]

The shifting political winds in America brought on by the rise of the nativist movement and the intensification of the slavery issue in the western territories ignited by the Kansas-Nebraska Act served as the backdrop for the creation of a new political party. The new Republican Party had varying success, depending on geographic region, in freeing itself from the stigma of nativism. The editor of the *Literary Budget* was thirty-four-year-old William W. Dannehower, who soon became the statewide leader of the Illinois nativist movement but also an eventual political ally and friend of Abraham Lincoln. Lincoln no doubt opposed nativism, but when he needed to, he worked with nativists. Against this confusing backdrop, a group of Illinois abolitionists and nativists called an 1854 meeting in Springfield to create a Republican Party and succeeded mainly in frightening away Lincoln and other moderate politicians afraid of being linked to extremists.

The new party was not successfully launched in Illinois until 1856.[3]

From the beginning Lincoln was wary of political contamination through association with the Know Nothing movement. When he was approached in the summer of 1854 by a committee of several local Know Nothings, among them Richard H. Ballinger and a Mr. Walgamot, who claimed to represent the true native American sentiment and sought to endorse him, Lincoln, the attorney, proceeded to cross examine them. Lincoln stated that "he had belonged to the old Whig party and must continue to do so until a better one arose to take its place," recalled Ballinger. Questioning Mr. Walgamot about who were the real native Americans, Lincoln asked, "Do they not wear breech-clout and carry tomahawk?" Lincoln continued by declaring, "We pushed them from their homes and now turn upon others not fortunate enough to come over as early as our forefathers." He informed them that "he could not become identified with the American Party—they might vote for him if they wanted to; so might the Democrats," but "he was not in sentiment with this new party." "Gentlemen of the committee," Lincoln concluded, "your party is wrong in principle."

Ballinger remembered that the conversation had lasted some time and that he had "wished many times before Mr. Lincoln was through that [he] had refused to serve on the committee." Describing Lincoln's demeanor, Ballinger said that the prairie lawyer's "great, half melancholy, half sympathetic face was frequently lighted up and almost put one into a trance. The kindly twinkle of the eye, the attractive smile told us there was more he wanted to say." And in vintage Lincoln fashion, he shared a humorous story to illustrate his points to the chastised gentlemen. "When the Know-nothing party first came up, I had an Irishman, Patrick by name, hoeing in my garden. One morning I was there with him, and he said, 'Mr. Lincoln, what about the Know-nothings?' I explained that they would possibly carry a few elections and disappear, and I asked Pat why he was not born in this country. 'Faith, Mr. Lincoln,' he replied, 'I wanted to be, but my mother wouldn't let me.'"[4]

Like Lincoln, the Irish and the Germans were wary of the new Republican Party and generally stayed away from it. Many Germans only halfheartedly went along or stressed that antislavery was the overriding issue in national politics, but temperance could be an important local or state issue. Germans therefore sent up warnings as Republicans prepared to organize in Illinois in 1856. At an Illinois newspaper editors' meeting held in Decatur during a fierce snowstorm in February, George Schneider of the *Illinois Staats-Zeitung* cautioned that Germans needed assurances that the new party had no connections with the Know Nothings. The editors drew up a platform that attacked the Kansas-Nebraska Act, called for the maintenance of the Missouri Compromise line of 36°30' to limit slavery's growth, and assured that slavery would not be touched where it already existed. Schneider then asked the newsmen to add another resolution, coming out for religious tolerance and the continuance of existing naturalization laws. Meeting with vehement opposition, Schneider asked for the opinion of the only politician who had braved the weather and was present, Abraham Lincoln. According to Schneider's later recollection, Lincoln responded that the resolution was not new, but was already contained in the Declaration of Independence. You cannot, Lincoln added, "form a new party on proscriptive principles." Humbled by Lincoln's remarks, the editors then endorsed Schneider's resolution, thereby castigating the Know Nothings publicly and establishing the immigrants as a crucial component of the new organization.[5]

A further warning came from Illinois lieutenant governor Gustave Koerner (also spelled Gustav or Gustavus Körner), a German Democrat who was preparing to leave his party if, as expected, its 1856 national convention pledged support for Stephen Douglas's Kansas-Nebraska Act. In many ways Koerner was the single most important German Lincoln ever befriended. Although he had entered Lincoln's world in June 1835, when Koerner rode the sixty-five miles from Belleville to Vandalia for his Illinois bar examination, he wrote about Lincoln for the first time five years later, when the Democratic stronghold of Belleville was invaded by the Whigs during the Log Cabin Campaign of 1840. Accompanying the Whigs at that time was Abraham Lincoln, who had gone along to stump for presidential candidate William Henry Harrison. The crowd was small, observed

Koerner, and "no doubt this disappointment had its effect upon Mr. Lincoln, who seemed rather depressed and was less happy with his remarks than usual. He sought to make much of the point that he had seen in Belleville that morning a fine horse sold by a constable for the price of twenty-seven dollars, and all due to the hard times produced by the Democrats. He was somewhat nonplused by the constable, who was in the crowd, crying out that the horse had but one eye." Koerner could not remember how Lincoln "got out of this scrape," but he did recall that "no one in the crowd could have dreamed that he was one day to be President."[6]

Lincoln and Koerner crossed paths many times after the German became an Illinois Supreme Court judge. Lincoln had argued many cases before Koerner, and the German immigrant observed that the court "always admired [Lincoln's] extreme fairness in stating his adversary's case as well as his own, and the often quaint and droll language used by him." When Lincoln returned to Belleville in 1856 to campaign for John C. Frémont, Koerner remembered that Lincoln "spoke in almost a conversational tone but with such earnestness and such deep feeling upon the question of the day that he struck the hearts of all hearers. Referring to the fact that here, as well as in other places where he had spoken, he had found the Germans more enthusiastic for the cause of freedom than all nationalities, he almost with tears in his eyes, broke out in the words: 'God bless the Dutch.' Everybody felt that he said this in the simplicity of his heart, using the familiar name of Dutch as the Americans do when amongst themselves. A smart politician would not have failed to say 'Germans.' But no one took offense."[7]

In a widely published letter to the Republican State Central Committee, Koerner stated that if he joined the new Republican Party, it would have to support the philosophy that "all American citizens without distinction of birth and religion should be entitled to rule America" and naturalization laws "should not be modified in an illiberal spirit." Lincoln was moved by this sentiment and used his influence when the Republicans met to approve a resolution vowing to "proscribe no one, by legislation or otherwise, on account of religious opinions, or in consequence of place of birth." With

Lincoln's support, the Illinois Republicans also nominated a German, Francis A. Hoffman of Chicago, as their party's candidate for lieutenant governor.

The Know Nothings may have lost out on the resolution debates, but their widely noted presence within the new Republican organizations placed the immigrant question at the center of the 1856 political campaigns in Illinois and the Midwest. Know Nothing successes in elections, both local and national, were mixed at best. Still, they achieved enough successes to startle those who found their platforms frightening. When Lincoln ran against Stephen Douglas in 1858 for the US Senate seat from Illinois, he was sufficiently concerned about nativism to write to his old friend and ally Koerner, "I learn that we are in great danger in Madison. It is said that half the Americans [Know Nothings] are going for Douglas; and the slam will ruin us if not counteracted. . . . We must make a special job of Madison. Every edge must be made to cut. Can not you, [Theodore] Canisius, and some other influential Germans set a plan on foot that shall gain us accessions from the Germans, and see that, at the election, none are cheated out of their ballots? [Representative Joseph] Gillespie thinks that thing is sometimes practiced on the Germans in Madison. . . . Nothing must be left undone." Koerner was sufficiently impressed to reply to his German brethren, "We must make them understand Lincoln is our man."[8]

Democrats tried to lure Germans away from Lincoln by spreading charges that he was secretly a Know Nothing and therefore anti-German. They inspired one German-born citizen, Dr. W. J. Wackerle of Meredosia, in Morgan County, Illinois, to publicly accuse Lincoln of Know Nothing associations and prejudices. On October 18, 1858, Lincoln angrily denied the charge at Meredosia. Indeed, the *Jacksonville Sentinel* reported that "Mr. Lincoln referred to the charge [made by Wackerle] and retorted to the Dr. in a severe, personal manner." But that was not the end of it. "I understand the story is being told, and insisted upon, that I have been a Know Nothing," Lincoln wrote to Edward Lusk, a farmer in Meredosia. "I repeat, what I have stated in a public speech at Meredosia, that I am not, nor have ever been, connected with the party called the Know-Nothing party, or party calling themselves the American party. *Certainly* no man of truth, and I *believe* no man [of] good character for truth can be found to say on his own knowledge that I ever was connected with that party."[9]

Lincoln lost the senatorial election to Douglas, but in many ways, although he had lost that battle, he had won the war. Better things were ahead for him, and his relationship with the German voters would play a significant role in his future. Koerner was impressed with Lincoln's performance in the debates. "When he [was] aroused," Koerner described Lincoln, "he appeared like a prophet of old. There came from Lincoln occasionally flashes of genius and burning words, revelations as it were from the unknown that will live as long as the English language lives." For, of all the immigrant groups in the United States, Lincoln preferred the Germans, according to his law partner William Herndon, who knew him intimately. Less than two years after Lincoln's death, Herndon gave an interview in Springfield to the famous correspondent George A. Townsend. In that little-known but quite revealing interview, published in the *New York Tribune* on February 15, 1867, Herndon recalled of Lincoln, "He had no prejudices against any class, preferring the Germans to any foreign element, yet tolerating—as I never could—even the Irish."

Lincoln despised the proscriptive principles of the Know Nothings and said so repeatedly in private. His public denunciations were fewer and quieter because many of his personal and political friends in Springfield had joined the Know Nothings and because the Republicans clearly needed their support to defeat the Democrats. To walk the political tightrope, Lincoln refused to accept that American citizenship was an inherited status; rather, it was something that could be obtained easily by embracing the principles of freedom that were the country's true foundation.

Lincoln's speech on the Fourth of July 1858 poignantly asserted that recent immigrants arriving in the United States should certainly feel as if the Declaration of Independence included them. It made no difference to Lincoln whether the immigrants had ancestors in America or not; the ideals of the Declaration belonged to them all. "We have besides these men—descended by blood from our ancestors," Lincoln emphasized, "among us perhaps half our people who are not descendants at all of these men, they are men who have come from Europe—German, Irish, French and Scandinavian—men that have come from Europe themselves, or whose ancestors have come hither and settled here, finding themselves our equals in all things. If they look back through this history to trace their connection with those days by blood, they find they have none, they cannot carry themselves back into that glorious epoch and make themselves feel that they are part of us, but when they look through that old Declaration of Independence they find that those old men say that 'We hold these truths to be self-evident, that all men are created equal,' and then they feel that that moral sentiment taught in that day evidences their relation to those men, that it is the father of all moral principle in them, and that they have a right to claim it as though they were blood of the blood, and flesh of the flesh of the men who wrote that Declaration, and so they are."[10]

In 1859, some months after Lincoln's loss to Douglas in the senatorial election, the state of Massachusetts adopted an amendment to its constitution that was regarded as strongly anti-immigrant. It provided for a residence period of two years after citizenship before the foreign-born could vote. Because the measure had been supported by Republicans in Massachusetts, Lincoln feared that his party would be labeled anti-immigrant, even in his own section of the nation. Such a label might mean defeat for Republican candidates in Illinois and other midwestern states, since the Republican and Democratic parties were about equally divided in voting strength. The worried Lincoln vented his concern in a letter to Schuyler Colfax of Indiana on July 6, 1859. "The point of danger," Lincoln wrote, "is the temptation in different localities to '*platform*' for something which will be popular just there, but which nevertheless, will be a firebrand elsewhere, and especially in a National convention." He continued, "What is desirable, if possible is that in every local convocation of Republicans, a point should be made to avoid everything which will distract republicans elsewhere. Massachusetts republicans should have looked beyond their noses; and then they could not have failed to see that tilting against foreigners would ruin us in the whole North-West."[11]

The Massachusetts resolution created a panic among Lincoln and his fellow Illinois Republicans. The *Chicago Press and Tribune* was the first noteworthy expression of opposition to the Massachusetts resolution. "Good faith and fair dealing," wrote the editors, "with those who separated themselves from the bogus Democracy to assist the party of Freedom in the accomplishment of the results which it proposes—who have for the sake of principle been willing to fraternize with the Know Nothings, their most deadly enemies—and who have, in their action on national questions at issue between parties, displayed a degree of patriotism and fidelity, which many an American might imitate with advantage—good faith to these demands that there should be no hesitation, no dodging, no compromise in this thing. It must be killed, or Republicanism in all the Northwestern States and not a few of the eastern states is needlessly and imminently imperiled!"[12] This editorial was widely quoted, and it was unquestionably one of the most influential expressions in the furious discussion that immediately swept over the country. Shortly after its publication, the *Springfield Daily Illinois State Journal* followed suit and denounced the Massachusetts measure in a column titled "Massachusetts' Constitution—Shameful Attempt at Proscription." Lincoln was caught in a whirlwind of activity and opposition over the events in Massachusetts, and he feverishly worked to keep both the Republican Party and his own political ambitions afloat in the face of the poisonous taint of Know Nothingism.

Nearby, the *Dubuque (Iowa) Daily Express and Herald*, one of the most influential Democratic newspapers in the Midwest, took no small degree of satisfaction in the Republicans' dilemma. "Their alarm is awful, their fright is complete, and they are 'running scared to death,'" crowed the paper. "It now seems to be at its highest pitch, and the whole brood of Republican leaders from Lincoln down . . . are uttering their disclaimers, issuing letters deprecatory and denunciative, and presenting to the mind's eye the picture of a hundred howling curs in the same predicament as . . . [a] panic stricken dog. Well, it is none of our funeral."[13]

To forestall the momentum and political capital being gained by the Democrats, Illinois Republicans conducted a series of meetings all over the state to register their disdain at any hints of association with the Know Nothing Party. At one such meeting Lincoln sent his law partner, William Herndon, to speak out against the Massachusetts resolution. "I conclude as I began," Herndon asserted at the end of his lengthy speech, "and by this principle [of democracy] I am willing to live or die—freedom and justice to all men—born, Protestant or Catholic; and may the chains of universal or partial despotism on mind or body—on individual or the race, be shivered and broken and snapt; and ring out loud and long. . . . Once an American citizen, always an American citizen."[14]

Shortly thereafter, the Illinois German newspapers threatened to abandon the Republican Party because of the Massachusetts resolution. Lincoln's old friend Gustave Koerner wrote to Lincoln and others seeking assistance in getting the Illinois Republican committee to pass a resolution denouncing the act. Lincoln was called upon to author the resolution, which he did. Writing on May 17, 1859, to Theodore Canisius, another German friend and editor of the German newspaper Lincoln would soon buy, the *Illinois Staats-Anzeiger*, Lincoln made it clear that he deplored the Massachusetts decision: "Massachusetts is a sovereign and independent state, and it is no privilege of mine to scold her for what she does. . . . [But] I say, then, that as I understand the Massachusetts provisions, I am against it's [*sic*] adoption in Illinois, or in any other place, where I have a right to oppose it. Understanding the spirit of our institutions to aim at the *elevation* of men, I am opposed to whatever tends to *degrade* them. I have some little notoriety for commiserating the oppressed condition of the negro; and I should be strangely inconsistent if I could favor any project for curtailing the existing rights of *white men*, even though born in different lands, and speaking different languages from myself."[15]

Canisius was both a faithful reporter and a very good friend, because he published Lincoln's letter in his newspaper and sent it along to the *Illinois State Journal*, where it was reprinted. "This letter," wrote Canisius in the note he attached, "[by] one of the gallant champions of our State is in accordance with the views of the whole German population, supporting the Republican party, and also with the views of the entire German Republican press. . . . We are glad Mr. Lincoln has written this letter. It is plain, straightforward and directly to the point. It contains not one word too much, neither does it omit anything of importance. Mr. Lincoln occupied the same ground as does the entire Republican party of the nation, and his letter will meet with their cordial concurrence and sympathy." Gustave Koerner appreciatively took note of Lincoln's support. "Amongst all the friends and admirers of Lincoln, none were more ardent and eager than the German Republicans," Koerner wrote Canisius, "the very name of Lincoln seemed to have a charm in it." Less than two weeks later Lincoln made a deal with Canisius to purchase the *Illinois Staats-Anzeiger*.[16]

Unfortunately, not a single copy of this newspaper exists today. It is estimated that the paper was published for approximately fifteen months between 1859 and 1861. And the Abraham Lincoln Presidential Library and Museum reported in 2011 that "a number of members of the 1861 Illinois General Assembly subscribed to the *Staats-Anzeiger* at state expense, as legislators were allowed. On February 23, 1861, the state auditor issued warrant #9297 (for $312) to Theodore Canisius for 312 copies of the *Staats-Anzeiger* for members of the state Senate; [and] #9309 (for $92) to Theodore Canisius for 240 copies of the *Staats-Anzeiger* for the House." Whether or not the paper continued past the November 1860 election, which saw Lincoln win a large number of German American votes, "at least 500 copies a week were sent to elected officials, most likely for distribution to voters in their districts."[17]

Lincoln's letter in the *Staats-Anzeiger* spawned other letters from fellow Republicans attempting to distance themselves from the Massachusetts resolution and any whiff of Know Nothingism. There was a flurry of activity among the Republicans in Illinois, with Lincoln leading the charge. In May 1859 the intensity of public interest in the Massachusetts two-year amendment among the electorate of Illinois was evident in the unprecedented number of letters, editorials, and reprints published in all the newspapers, German and English alike. But it was Lincoln's letter that attracted an inordinate amount of attention. A cautious politician by nature, Lincoln was not much given to public letter writing and, on principle, studiously avoided committing his views on such matters to print in a newspaper. He knew full well the political fatalities that could befall an aspiring candidate by launching "effusive epistolary declarations," as one contemporary newspaper described them. Lincoln was acutely concerned that the timing of his statement would be opportune, and given the danger of mistiming its publication amid the vast changes in politics and the constant shifting of public interest in the 1850s, a misstep could be politically fatal. Therefore, the situation must have seemed urgent enough to Lincoln that he felt it was necessary to pen this letter to the Springfield committee of Germans.

One political observer, F. I. Herriott, pointed to the Lincoln letter as "a model of conciseness and lucidity, pith and point." Unlike so many of his fellow Republicans, Lincoln stayed on point and did not make "ugly implications." "His language neither burns nor scars," wrote Herriott, "yet it is luminous and flashes far and wide a principle of human equality that critics could not deny and those for whom it was intended would greet with hearty applause." Lincoln stuck to the principles of equality and justice for the immigrants and did not seek to attack the Massachusetts Republicans for their actions. In the process, he provided Springfield Germans with exactly what they had asked for and what they needed.[18]

Lincoln's letter is evidence of the man as a surefooted lawyer, who is scrupulously observant of principle and realizes the fact that a right, when it exists, must compel respect for those exercising it. Thus he made his frank assertion that he did not have the right to "scold" the people of Massachusetts for their determination because it was their prerogative. Yet he also made it clear that he opposed the principle and policy of the Massachusetts amendment and that he would oppose its adoption in Illinois and in any federal jurisdiction wherever he had a legal right to do so.

Lincoln cleverly linked the antislavery movement with his opposition to the Massachusetts amendment. He referred to his "notoriety for commiserating the oppressed condition of the negro" and his opposition to "any project for curtaining the existing right of white men, even though born in different lands and speaking different languages from myself." This both met the demands of the protesting Germans and answered the most contemptuous denunciations of the Democrats, for it raised the crucial principles of the antislavery movement and prevented the opposition in Massachusetts from taking any just exception to the points made from Lincoln's argument.[19]

It is no surprise that Lincoln was guided in his opposition to the amendment by his basic principles and not by the prevailing winds of popular prejudice and passion or the turbulent gusts of popular fancy or fury. Certainly this was the case when it came to Lincoln and the Know Nothings. A letter to his closest friend, Joshua Speed, four years earlier, the source of his ubiquitous quote, expressed the same sentiment as that expressed in his well-circulated letter to Theodore Canisius. "I am not a Know-Nothing. That is certain," Lincoln declared in 1855. "How could I be? How can any one who abhors the oppression of negroes, be in favor of degrading classes of white people?" But Lincoln did not stop there. "Our progress in degeneracy appears to be pretty rapid. As a nation, we began by declaring that *all men are created equal*.' We now practically read it 'all men are created equal except *negroes*.' When the Know-Nothings get control, it will read 'all men are created equal, except negroes *and foreigners, and Catholics*.' When it comes to this I should prefer emigrating to some country where they make no pretense of loving liberty—to Russia for instance, where despotism can be taken pure, and without the base alloy of hypocracy [*sic*]."[20] At the same time, Lincoln wrote to Owen Lovejoy, "I have no objection to 'fuse' with anybody provided I can fuse on ground which I think is right and I believe the opponents of slavery extension could now do this, if it were not for this K[now]-N[othing]ism." It is apparent, then, that Lincoln was not merely attempting to placate the Germans with his letter to Canisius on May 17, 1859, since his opinion had been formed at least four years earlier, in the midst of "Bleeding Kansas" and the fanatical sectionalism, discord, violence, and bloodshed that dominated there.[21]

Lincoln was also quite straightforward in his letter to Canisius about the "fusion" of the Republicans "with the other opposition elements for the canvass of 1860." Lincoln took pains to explain to the anxious Germans, fearful that the Republicans would fuse with the Know Nothings, "As to the matter of fusion, I am for it, if it can be had on republican grounds; and I am not for it on any other terms. A fusion on any other terms would be as foolish as unprincipled. It would lose the whole North, while the common enemy would still carry the whole South. The question of *men* is a different one. There are good patriotic men, and able statesmen, in the South whom I would cheerfully support, if they would now place themselves on republican ground. But I am against letting down the republican standard a hair's breath." Lincoln's old friend Gustave Koerner agreed with him. "It is time we should quit the absurd hope of gaining converts from the Know-Nothings," he wrote to Lincoln. "In our state they have taken their sides. They do not pretend to exist as a party. This policy [of appealing to the Know Nothings] pursued by some of our friends . . . has been from the very start fatal to us. For every Know-nothing we gained we lost two Republicans."[22]

Still, other Republicans continued to fret over the need to attract more Know Nothing voters. Lincoln remained firm and reminded his fellow Republicans of his unwillingness to make concessions, warning that "the only danger will be the temptation to lower the Republican Standard in order to gather recruits." "In my judgment," he continued, "such a step would be a serious mistake—would open a gap through which more would pass *out* than pass *in*. And this would be the same, whether the letting down should be in deference to [Know Nothingism], or to the southern opposition element. Either would surrender the object of the Republican organization. . . . That object surrendered; the organization would go to pieces." Shortly thereafter, in a speech at Clinton, Illinois, Lincoln signaled that the time had passed to be concerned about the Know Nothing question. The Know Nothing Party "was in existence [in 1856], but now that organization was absorbed into both the other great parties, and . . . *now*, and only *now*, we could rejoice over a true and genuine Republican triumph."[23]

Nevertheless, two fellow Republicans wrote to Lincoln reiterating the need for the party to rid itself of any stigma of the old Know Nothing prejudices: "Our party is a composite one and has diverse elements whose tastes and feelings ought to be carefully handled until time renders us a homogenous mass. Such arguments, or rather such appeals to old prejudices that ought to be forgotten, only serve to perpetuate our original diversities and to retard very much the complete fusion which must take place before we can hope to become a power in the land."[24]

Lincoln's stance is all the more impressive given the relentless pressure that prominent newspaper editors like Horace Greeley were putting on the Republican Party to unite with the Know Nothings to defeat the Democrats. In fact, Greeley's *New York Tribune* went so far as to suggest in an editorial that the opponents of slavery consider the feasibility of a working alliance among the various factions of several political parties. This could be accomplished, Greeley maintained, by allowing the Republicans to nominate the candidate for vice president and allowing fusion party members such as the Know Nothings to select the candidate for president. After all, he asserted, there was no discernible difference between the former Whigs and the Know Nothings on the subject of slavery. Greeley's contention was that the new Republicans and the Know Nothings fused together would surely defeat any proslavery Democratic ticket in the impending presidential election of 1860.[25] Lincoln's characteristic candor and frankness in opposing the inclusion of the Know Nothings in the Republican Party elicited the applause of friends and the admiration of party opponents and political critics.[26]

Germans in Illinois and across the country were outraged by Greeley's editorial. A considerable majority of the German press, after the repeal of the Missouri Compromise by virtue of the Kansas-Nebraska Act, was radical and outspoken in its opposition to slavery—opposed to its extension and, indeed, opposed to its very existence. Many Germans had fled their former homelands in the wake of the Revolutions of 1848, and the new Fugitive Slave Act of 1850 and the Supreme Court's ruling in the Dred Scott decision in 1857 had reminded too many of these "Forty-Eighters" of the tyrannical and oppressive rule they had left behind. An alliance, or any formal affiliation, with the Know Nothing Party or the conservative former Whigs who opposed any interference with the rights of slaveholders was simply anathema to the Germans and other like-minded immigrants. And Lincoln knew this. Writing to a colleague, Lincoln acknowledged that "the inherent obstacle to any plan of union [with the Know Nothings] lies in the fact that [of] those [G]ermans we now have with us, large numbers will fall away, so soon as it is seen that their votes, cast with us, may possibly be used to elevate Mr. Fillmore," the Know Nothing candidate.[27]

The German editors recalled vividly the Know Nothing Party's rabid persecutions and felt that Greeley's editorials suggesting the practicality of supporting such latecomer politicians as Edward Bates, John Bell, or John M. Botts as fusion candidates within the new Republican Party were not only unacceptable but insulting. "These men," wrote one German editor, "stood foremost in the country as sanctioning narrow, proscriptive legislation by their silence, if not by speech, giving countenance to the brutalities of Know-nothingism." To the Germans, what Greeley proposed was an unholy alliance with the powers of evil, and it had prompted Theodore Canisius to write a letter to Lincoln asking point-blank whether he supported the fusion of the Republicans with "other Opposition elements for the canvass of 1860." Canisius and his conferees knew that there was intense and widespread opposition to fusion among staunch antislavery advocates, and they knew, too, that Lincoln was keenly aware of the intense feelings of the Germans in regard to anything that smacked of Know Nothingism.[28]

With Germans universally opposed to the Massachusetts two-year amendment, Lincoln did not hedge his bets with qualifying clauses that would enable him to hide behind political expediency. He would not accept the Know Nothings into his party, or anyone else for that matter, unless they accepted all the Republican principles and foundations for which he stood. However, Lincoln made it abundantly clear that he would follow the lead of any experienced standard-bearer whose character would inspire confidence and afford the greatest hope of victory. And he clearly asserted that he would "cheerfully support" a number of "good and patriotic men of the South" if they would "place themselves on Republican ground." Clearly then, in a significant departure from the German stated preference, Lincoln would support the candidacy of Edward Bates, John Bell, John Botts, or Simon Cameron should any of them be nominated as the Republican presidential nominee in 1860. To some, Lincoln's stand was either a most daring and reckless assertion of independence or an act of supreme wisdom and perfect politics. In the art of politics or prudence, the wily prairie lawyer was a grand master, and his ability and achievement were never more effectively demonstrated than in his response to Canisius and his colleagues.[29]

While the German press was effusive in its reaction to Lincoln's stand on the Massachusetts amendment, at no time before the Republican convention met in Chicago in May 1860 did they ever indicate any agreement in support of the candidacies of Bell, Bates, and Botts. The candidate name they bandied about was that of pro-immigrant William Seward from New York. They treated the candidacy of nativist-minded Edward Bates with either contemptuous silence or downright denunciation, despite Lincoln's apparent willingness to support him should he be the nominee. German hostility steadily increased until March 1860, when it became an outright organized movement that ultimately derailed the Bates candidacy.

Lincoln's debates with Stephen Douglas the previous year had made him a national figure in the mainstream press. The German press and its reaction to his letter to Theodore Canisius made him a favorite among Germans and other like-minded immigrant groups. Shortly thereafter, antislavery and Republican papers began to suggest him for consideration at the forthcoming national convention as a suitable candidate for either of the two places on the national ticket. At the time Lincoln wrote Canisius, the national committee had not yet selected Chicago as the place of meeting, and ardent westerners not only were looking for the meeting to take place west of the Appalachian Mountains but also hoped for one of their own to secure a place on the November ballot. Lincoln fit that bill.

Essential to any Republican success was the harmonious coalescing of nativists and foreign-born constituents within the antislavery coalition. Though seemingly incompatible, both groups had supported Lincoln in his 1858 campaign against Stephen Douglas. And now Lincoln's genius was in his ability to present himself as acceptable to two such factions while not compromising his principles or ignoring the political pressure of the Germans and other immigrant groups. In so doing, he would ensure a united effort for himself and his party. Lincoln refused to panic over the nativist threat, as did other antislavery leaders, who either rushed to make concessions to the Know Nothings or attacked nativism in impolitic fervor. As 1860 approached, Lincoln adroitly maneuvered through the political minefield of how to combine discordant factions into a single coalition, always careful not to alienate the Know Nothings but never conceding to the nativist issues, which would offend the immigrants.

So concerned with the German support was Lincoln that he accepted an invitation to go on a speaking tour in Kansas, in part because of the Germans' insistence that he was needed there. John P. Hatterscheidt, as leader of the German Republican community in Leavenworth, Kansas, extended the invitation to what only a few years before had been a virulently proslavery town. But German immigration to Leavenworth had transformed the town into a free labor community. No other town in Kansas had such a high concentration of Germans, who represented more than 30 percent of its population. Champion Vaughan, the editor of the *Leavenworth Daily Times*, acknowledged the new German reality when he wrote, "The Germans are a power here. They are Republicans and it is their right to be fairly represented in the party." Not stopping there, Vaughan, formerly of Cincinnati, where German Americans represented a significant presence, declared, "We go one step further. As a matter of feeling and principle, we should so deal with them. For what is the basis of emancipation in Missouri and Texas? On what does it rest, chiefly in all the slave states? On the German element! It is for free soil without compromise, and for free labor without qualification or disguise. We stand by the Germans, then on principle, because they are men of principle."[30] And now the Germans needed Lincoln to come and support them.

Lincoln left for Kansas in early December 1859 and agreed to give speeches in Troy, Doniphan, Atchison, and Leavenworth. Hatterscheidt headed the welcoming committee when Lincoln arrived in

Troy, and even though many Germans were still touting the presidential candidacy of William Seward, the German community in Kansas took Lincoln very seriously as a representative of their interests on a national stage. A German band greeted Lincoln upon his arrival in Leavenworth, and a parade accompanied him into town.[31]

"All those who believe that slavery is wrong," Lincoln told the Kansans, "should unite on a policy, dealing with it as a wrong. They should be deluded into no deceitful contrivances, pretending indifference, but really working for that to which they are opposed." Two days later, Lincoln acknowledged the trials of the Kansans to make their land the home of the free and reiterated that this was also his cause as well as that of the Republicans. Lincoln's second speech concluded with a forceful definition of the aims and principles of the Republican Party. He showed how the Republicans "harmonized" with the teachings of the founders. Their success, he said, was "essential to the proper development of our country—its progress and its glory—to the salvation of the Union and the perpetuity of Free Institutions."[32]

Lincoln was well received by the Kansas Germans, as reports in the press indicate. "His short stay in Kansas has been full of significance," said the *Leavenworth Daily Times*. "He has met a reception that would be accorded to but a few in the nation, and he has sown seed that cannot but be productive of great good. We part with him regretfully, and we echo but the sentiments of our people when we wish for him a long life and honors befitting such a gallant captain in the army of freedom. Abe Lincoln came to us no stranger but his presence, and his words have drawn him closer to our hearts. He is our friend—the friend of Kansas—and he will ever find the latchstring out when he may choose to honor us with another visit. Full of gratitude for services rendered, of admiration for his heroic qualities, we bid honest Abe a kind and heartfelt farewell."[33]

Even though this Kansas appreciation for Lincoln did not translate into a serious challenge to Seward as the German Kansans' favorite candidate, newspapers in nearby Iowa advised the German Republicans to take note that Lincoln would be "one of the candidates for which Illinois would ask the electors to vote for President."[34] In and around Springfield, the Germans, Portuguese, Jews, and even some Irish, joined in the growing chorus for Lincoln to be a national candidate. Lincoln was well aware of this, for he was duly informed by friends and supporters almost on a daily basis. Back in 1856 he had received 110 votes for vice president when the Republican Party was in its infancy. Now, as the presidential election loomed on the horizon, Lincoln was receiving encouragement from the immigrant groups with whom he had harmoniously coexisted since coming to Springfield many years before.

Looking toward the nominating convention, Lincoln wrote from Indiana to Schuyler Colfax, arguably one of the most prominent Republican leaders in Congress, about "the movement against foreigners in Massachusetts; in New Hampshire, to make obedience to the fugitive slave law punishable as a crime; in Ohio, to repeal the fugitive slave law; and squatter sovereignty, in Kansas," saying, "In these things there is explosive matter enough to blow up a dozen national conventions, if it gets into them, and what gets very rife outside of conventions is very likely to find its way into them. . . . In a word, in every locality we should look beyond our noses; and at least say nothing on points where it is probable we shall disagree. . . . If you see danger as I think I do, [I hope] you will do what you can to avert it. Could not suggestions be made to leading men in the State and Congressional conventions, and so avoid, to some extent, at least these apples of discord?"[35] Lincoln was assuming a leadership role, and his clear, lucid, and convincing prose about the issues facing the Republicans proved to be prophetic.

While the issue of slavery and the Union dominated the attention of virtually everyone, Lincoln being no exception, his bold entrance into those issues concerning the immigrants and their antipathy toward the Know Nothing Party attracted national attention. And this provided momentum for his political aspirations, for much of the political maneuvering for 1860 still centered on the parties' real or alleged relationships with the Know Nothings. This development revealed the growing importance of the immigrant vote. Local conventions of both parties would soon require delegates to stand and pledge that they had no sympathy with the Know Nothings. Lincoln's longtime nemesis Stephen Douglas thrived on the nativism stories, pointing out eagerly to anyone who would listen the presence of Know Nothings in the Republican Party and warning that the "white basis" of American government would suffer if black and immigrant equality was forced upon the nation.

Germans feared the power of the eastern Republicans and the possibility that the national convention in 1860 might take some step similar to Massachusetts that would frighten away the immigrants. In an effort to forestall such a development, a group of Illinois German Republicans, led by Gustave Koerner and Carl Schurz, called a preconvention gathering in 1860 at the Deutsches Haus in Chicago. The structure itself had become a symbol of immigrant resistance since its construction in 1856 to provide a German meeting place during the Know Nothing rise to power. With its ranks including leading Forty-Eighters and a heavy sprinkling of German editors, the Deutsches Haus gathering drew up resolutions endorsing a free Kansas and a homestead act, and repudiating the Massachusetts amendment. The German resolution stated bluntly, "The Republican party is opposed to any change in our naturalization laws, or any state legislation, by which the rights of citizenship heretofore accorded to immigrants from foreign lands will be abridged or impaired, and is in favor of giving full and sufficient protection to all classes of citizens, whether native or naturalized, both home and abroad." The Germans presented this as a deal-breaking resolution to the Republican convention, with noted German leader Carl Schurz warning that three hundred thousand German votes hung in the balance. The convention adopted the "Dutch plan" unanimously, despite some efforts by the Massachusetts delegates to block it.[36]

Lincoln was among the first to fully appreciate the importance of the German vote and the equal significance of the nativist movement and what they portended for the Republican Party, since both accounted for more in Lincoln's party and the antislavery movement than they did with the Democratic opponents. His political savvy served him well, and his foreign-born friends soon demonstrated their support on his behalf. After the adoption of the "Dutch plan," the Republicans went about selecting their nominee for president.

Three contenders for the nomination were of especial interest to the Germans and other immigrant groups. Senator William Seward of New York, with an impressive antinativist record and open advocacy of a homestead bill, was to many the front runner. But Seward was unacceptable to any nativist Republicans. Missouri's Edward Bates, a conservative Free-Soiler who had supported Know Nothing candidates and presided over the last Know Nothing Party national convention, was not in any way acceptable to the immigrants. Abraham Lincoln, on the other hand, seemed to be the best of all worlds, moderate yet with strongly held principles. Managers for the New York senator, the Missouri judge, and the Illinois lawyer worked feverishly to line up delegates for their men.

At the opening of the convention, the German Republicans supported Seward but were ready to use any means necessary to stop Bates should Seward fail to secure the nomination. Stopping Bates became even more crucial as it became apparent that Seward did not have the delegates to take a first-round victory. Lincoln's name was bandied about all the more among the Germans as Seward's star seemed to be falling. Shortly before the Republican National Convention convened, the *Turn-Zeitung* of Baltimore, the central organ of the German Turnerbund of the United States, an organization dedicated to German social, athletic, and political well-being, stated, "If on the score of expediency we passed Mr. Seward by, then . . . [may] Mr. Lincoln be [our] man."[37]

Former Illinois lieutenant governor Gustave Koerner was one of Lincoln's main strategists at the convention, and he worked closely with two other old friends of Lincoln, Judge David Davis and Illinois Republican state chairman Norman B. Judd, to secure Lincoln's nomination. The three went among the delegates from voter-rich states such as Pennsylvania and Indiana, preaching the anti-Bates, pro-Lincoln gospel. Bates was soon ruled out because his conservative views did not satisfy the antislavery forces and because his former political nativism was unacceptable to the Germans and similar-minded immigrant voters. With both Lincoln and Seward acceptable to the Germans, Carl Schurz, leading the Wisconsin delegation, favored Seward until it became obvious that the New Yorker did not have the requisite number of delegates to secure the nomination through the first several ballots. Considerations of expediency, moderation, and electability, not to mention the skillful machinations behind the scenes by Lincoln's managers, ultimately secured the top spot for the former rail-splitter.

At crucial points in the Republican nomination process, the aggressive German American movement to defeat Edward Bates's candidacy opened the path for the initiatives of Lincoln's managers to win such key states as Pennsylvania and Ohio in a series of "well planned and boldly executed" maneuvers. These behind-the-scenes eleventh-hour successes on the part of the Germans brought about Seward's unlikely defeat and Lincoln's unexpected and dramatic nomination for the presidency.[38]

Lincoln remained in Springfield during the ensuing campaign, taking the necessary steps to ensure that the majority of German and immigrant votes remained safe for himself and other Republican candidates. Immediately after the convention, formerly pro-Seward Carl Schurz, in his capacity as a member of the National Republican Committee in charge of the foreign department, wrote to Lincoln proposing a list of all "Germans, Norwegians, Hollanders, etc., who can serve our cause in the way of public speaking." He planned to organize the immigrants into squads to send out to contested states in the belief that the foreign vote of 1856 could be doubled in the North, and before doing so, he wished to consult with Lincoln.[39] "I am much mortified that I did not attend to your letter at once," Lincoln apologized. "I . . . glanced over it too hastily to properly appreciate its importance, laid it by and it passed from my mind, till Gov. Koerner mentioned it to-day. . . . I hope you have gone forward on your plan without my advice. To me it appears an excellent plan; and I have no sufficient experience to suggest any improvement to it." In a nod to Schurz's importance, Lincoln vowed, "And now, upon this bad beginning, you must not determine to write me no more; for I promise you, that no letter of yours to me, shall ever again be neglected." In his truest sense as a politician, Lincoln sought to mitigate any fears Schurz might entertain that hard feelings existed between the two in the aftermath of the recently completed convention. "I beg you to be assured," Lincoln wrote, "that your having supported Gov. Seward, in preference to myself in the convention, is not even remembered by me for any practical purpose, or the slightest unpleasant feeling. I go not back to the convention, to make distinctions among its members; and, to the extent of our limited acquaintance, no man stands nearer my heart than yourself."[40]

Schurz plunged enthusiastically into the presidential campaign against Lincoln's three opponents, Stephen Douglas, John Bell, and John C. Breckinridge. In July, when Schurz was Lincoln's guest in Springfield, the two men were escorted with torches and orchestrated fanfare by American and German "Wide Awake" clubs, which were paramilitary campaign organizations replete with their own uniforms. Schurz even spoke to the crowd from the State House steps. A severe critic of Douglas, Schurz stated that as long as morality existed in the nation, Douglas and his cohorts would "in vain endeavor to reduce the people to that disgusting state of moral indifference" of which Douglas himself was not ashamed to boast. "However degraded some of our politicians may be," Schurz concluded, "the progress of the struggle will show that the popular conscience is still alive, and that people DO CARE." The speech was so successful that it was widely reprinted.[41] One of those most impressed with Schurz's speech was Lincoln, who this time took pains to write the German a letter of appreciation and congratulations.

Schurz began to stump for Lincoln and wrote to his wife that "the old 'Pennsylvania Dutch' follow me like children, although they can only half understand me. The Democrats are furious, and wherever I have spoken they telegraph like mad in all directions for German speakers to neutralize my speeches." Schurz had become so prominent that his portrait on *cartes de visite* was already being sold in New York stores. The Republican leaders knew that they owed him, and he was well aware that Lincoln would not forget him. But Schurz was not alone in his campaigning. Along with Schurz, the Republicans sent Germans and Jews to various ethnic enclaves, particularly in the old Northwest, and in the process, spent a considerable amount of money for their expenses.[42] Joining Schurz on the campaign trail were Gustave Koerner, Adolf Douai, Friedrich Hassaurek, John P.

Hatterscheidt, Johann Lutz Mannfield (John L. Mansfield), and a host of other German and Jewish immigrants.

Were Germans the crucial element in Lincoln's 1860 presidential victory? There is much disagreement on the answer to that question. A number of recent examinations of voting precincts indicate that Germans in Wisconsin and Iowa generally voted Democratic, retaining their former allegiance. Lincoln's loss in Missouri included defeat in some German areas. A similar electoral situation prevailed in Iowa, where Germans and Hollanders ignored their leaders and editors and returned to the Democratic fold, perhaps influenced by the Massachusetts question or the Republicans' identification with temperance. It was said that many of the Dutch in Iowa "were suspicious of the abolitionist elements in the new party." Among the Minnesota townships where more than half the population was made up of Germans, twelve went Republican and two went Democratic in 1860. German voters were important but not crucial in Lincoln's victory in that new state.

Lincoln's victory in Illinois included two major German centers: Chicago, where he received 58 percent of the total vote, and St. Clair County, which gave him almost 55 percent. In the latter case, it was reported that "in precinct after precinct a preponderance of Germans is always associated with a Lincoln majority." In all likelihood, 60 to 65 percent of the Republican German vote in Illinois went for Lincoln. Even if the German votes were not crucial in Lincoln's Illinois win, they were important in forcing Republicans to take stands that appealed to the immigrant. Efforts to win immigrant support joined with the immigrants' own increasing activism within the political system to create a vastly different political environment as the 1850s came to a close.

This change was evident when an Irishman wrote home from Chicago in 1860 that there was "the greatest kind of excitement" between Democrats and Republicans, "just what there would be prodestant and Catholick [sic]." And he described a rather simple political division: "All Catholics here is Democrat and for slavery and all Republicans is prodestants or not for slavery but it is not known yet which will beat." In the end, the final vote tally determined "which will beat." Lincoln's victory, determined in a large or small part by the Germans, Jews, Hollanders, and others, established a precedent. The campaign itself and the efforts by politicians to recruit the immigrant vote provide ample historical evidence that the significant numbers of immigrants who had arrived in the 1840s and 1850s had finally been drawn into the American political system. They were mere spectators no longer.[43]

Notwithstanding the present debate over the role of immigrants in Lincoln's election, the *New York Herald*, one of the nation's most widely circulated Democratic papers, observed one month after the election that "in Ohio, Illinois, Indiana, Iowa, and Wisconsin native Republicans now openly acknowledge that their victory was, if not wholly, at least to a great extent, due to the large accessions they received from the German ranks." And on his way to his inauguration, Lincoln paid homage to the immigrant vote he had received. Addressing a group of German mechanics in Cincinnati in February 1861, Lincoln offered one of his most definitive statements on the immigrant. "In regard to the Germans and foreigners," Lincoln asserted, "I esteem them no better than any other people, nor any worse. It is not in my nature, when I see a people borne down by the weight of their shackles—the oppression of tyranny—to make their life more bitter by heaping upon them greater burdens; but rather would I do all in my power to raise the yoke, than to add anything that would tend to crush them. Inasmuch as our country is extensive and new, and the countries of Europe are densely populated, if there is any abroad who desire to make this the land of their adoption, it is not in my heart to throw aught in their way to prevent them from coming to the United States."[44] Despite their status as recent immigrants, the Germans had set in motion a powerful "upsurge of moral enthusiasm and determination" for Lincoln, which he would not forget.

Lincoln was about to face the greatest challenge of his life and the life of the nation. That he would encounter issues and demands that distracted him from his interest in immigrant affairs goes without saying. Nevertheless, the immigrants and foreign-born would play important roles in his military, social, economic, and political programs. And this would begin almost immediately.

WISDOM: WHIG IN THE
WHITE HOUSE

Darkening war clouds on the horizon overshadowed the weather on Abraham Lincoln's fifty-second birthday. Seeking to pay homage to the immigrant group most significant in his recent election, Lincoln ventured to Cincinnati to address a sizable group of Germans. The Germans are "of the great family of men," the president-elect told them on February 12, 1861, "and if there is one shackle upon any of them, it would be far better to lift the load from them than to pile additional loads upon them. And inasmuch as the continent of America is comparatively a new country, and the other countries of the world are old countries, there is more room here, comparatively speaking than there is there; and if they can better their condition by leaving their old homes, there is nothing in my heart to forbid them coming; and I bid them all God speed."[1]

The Germans in particular celebrated Abraham Lincoln's election as if he were one of their own. And to some German Americans, he was. On the basis of an old Land Office warrant made out to his namesake grandfather, Abraham *Linkhorn*, the newly elected president possessed a perfectly acceptable Germanic name and surely one to justify their ongoing loyalty and support above and beyond all other immigrant groups.[2] Whether or not the Germans were as responsible for his election as they believed, Lincoln warmly welcomed them into his inner circle and would call on them throughout his administration in both a civilian and military capacity.

Before his inauguration, Lincoln sequestered himself away, meeting with his advisors. Lincoln's old friend and confidant Gustave Koerner was called to Springfield to help the newly elected Illinois governor, Richard Yates. Lincoln, who was spending many hours in the governor's office, found the time to discuss many issues with his old German friend. "I had an excellent opportunity of studying the character of the president-elect," Koerner recalled. "To be sure, we had been before on very friendly terms, but in more of a social and professional way than a political one." Thirty days after Lincoln's election South Carolina seceded, starting a procession of Southern states fleeing the Union. In all, seven Deep South states left, creating the Confederate States of America, before Lincoln even reached Washington, DC, for his inauguration. "As I was one of the few who took part in the various discussions of these startling events," Koerner wrote, "I was brought nearer to Lincoln than ever before. I cannot say there was any warm friendship between us. Lincoln, though one of the most just, kind, and indulgent of men, who intentionally I believe never did an unkind thing to anyone, was not in my opinion, as also in the opinion of others who knew him well, really capable of what might be called warm-hearted friendship. But I can say in truth, that I enjoyed his confidence to a very great extent."

This was no exaggeration. As Lincoln took the oath of office to become the nation's sixteenth president, Koerner was one of the individuals standing closest to him. "While the weather was fine, it was nevertheless quite cold on the platform," Koerner remembered. "Douglas had no overcoat, and I saw he was shivering. I had not only a big overcoat on but a thick traveling shawl, which I flung over him to make him comfortable. At several passages of Lincoln's inaugural, Douglas pressed my arm, saying, 'Good, good.' Yet only a few days afterwards he commented very severely on the speech, called it a declaration of war, and placed himself and all his friends in congress in opposition to the administration."[3]

Fellow German Carl Schurz, who feared that Lincoln might be too soft on slavery in his inaugural address, was invited by Lincoln to visit him in Springfield before the president-elect left for the nation's capital. While there, the German immigrant heard a preview of the inaugural address, "a mark of confidence which I have given to no other man," Lincoln told Schurz. After the two men had "discussed it point by point," Lincoln swore Schurz to secrecy, reminding him, "Now you know better than any other man in the country how I stand, and you may be sure that I shall never betray my principles and my friends."[4] Before the sixteenth president's administration even began in earnest, Lincoln's two German friends were front and center.

After his inauguration on March 4, 1861, President Lincoln found himself bedeviled by the onslaughts of office seekers. Carl Schurz had been promised the diplomatic post of US minister to Sardinia during one of his visits to Lincoln. Two weeks after his inauguration Lincoln wrote Secretary of State William H. Seward about diplomatic appointments: "This being done leaves but five full missions undisposed of—Russia, China, Brazil, Peru, & Chili [sic]. And, then, what about Carl Schurz? or, in other words, what about our German friends?"[5] Unlike Lincoln, Seward was in no hurry to appoint the president's German friends to diplomatic posts.

It was more than a year into the Lincoln administration before Schurz received the political reward he felt he deserved. He protested vehemently when he learned that Seward would prohibit foreign-born Americans from serving in diplomatic posts. "I need hardly inform you," Schurz wrote to Lincoln, "that this information which has not been contradicted and not disproved by an appointment of a naturalised citizen to such a mission, has created the most intense sensation amongst the German Republicans all through the country."[6]

Lincoln was quite willing to give the Sardinian mission to Schurz, but Seward opposed the appointment on the grounds that Schurz had been a revolutionary in Europe and might prove to be unacceptable to the Sardinian court. Lincoln was undeterred and resolved to take care of Schurz by appointing him US minister to Spain, even though that country was a monarchy as well, with no taste for revolutionaries. This, however, was not what Schurz ultimately wanted. Ever since the firing on Fort Sumter, Schurz had been contemplating a military career. By the end of 1861, bored and restless with the plush and easy life in his diplomatic position, and disturbed by the war news at home, Schurz pleaded with Lincoln to permit him to return home and join the army. It was because of his fierce determination to fight for the Union that Schurz obtained a three-month leave to raise cavalry regiments in New York. Thus, when he returned to the United States, his principal purpose was to secure a commission in the army.[7]

From the moment he arrived in Washington, Schurz used all of the political skills he possessed to secure his nomination. He headed to the White House to plead his case directly to Lincoln, stressing the fact that the Republicans needed to recognize the significance of the Germans. Unwilling to accept a token command, Schurz pressed his case to Lincoln for the appointment of a significant commission. There is little doubt that Lincoln would have preferred that Schurz return to Madrid, since the new president had his hands full on many fronts. And for weeks after meeting with Schurz, the president neither accepted his diplomatic resignation nor assigned him to a command position.

Finally, in June 1862, Schurz took command of a division in the corps of fellow German Franz Sigel and fought at Second Bull Run. The following March Schurz was promoted to major general in General Oliver O. Howard's corps. Schurz had temporary command in the corps at the Battle of Gettysburg, took part in the Battle of Chattanooga, and then joined Sherman on his March to the Sea. During the war, Schurz corresponded regularly with Lincoln, constantly making recommendations on the conduct of the war, often to the exasperation of the president.[8] He criticized Lincoln for Republican losses in the midterm elections of 1862, and Lincoln responded to Schurz in uncharacteristically sharp tones. "You think I could do better; therefore you blame me already," Lincoln wrote. "I think I could not do better; therefore I blame you for blaming me. I understand *you* now to be willing to accept the help of men who are not republicans, provided they have 'heart in it.' Agreed. I want no others. But who is to be the judge of hearts, or of 'heart in it'? If I must discard my own judgment, and take yours, I must also take that of others; and by the time I should reject all I should be advised to reject, I should have none left, republicans, or others—not even yourself. For, be assured, my dear sir, there are men who have 'heart in it' that think you are performing your part as poorly as you think I am performing mine."[9]

But overall Lincoln was quite generous in appointing his German friends to diplomatic posts: Friedrich Hassaurek of Cincinnati as minister to Ecuador, Charles N. Riotte of Texas as minister to Costa Rica, and Hermann Kreismann of Chicago as secretary of legation to the Hohenzollern court at Berlin. In addition to those appointments, Lincoln bestowed numerous American consulate posts on German American Republican leaders, including Dr. George E. Wiss of Maryland, born in Bavaria, consul at Rotterdam; George Schneider of Chicago, also from Bavaria, consul at Elsinore, Denmark; Lincoln's old partner in the German American newspaper, Theodore Canisius of Springfield, consul at Vienna; John P. Hatterscheidt of Kansas, Prussian-born, consul at Moscow; Charles L. Bernays of Missouri, a native of Hesse-Darmstadt, consul at Zurich; Henry Boernstein of Missouri, born in Hamburg, consul at Bremen; August L. Wolff of Iowa, native of Lippe-Detmold, consul at Basle; August Alers of California, originally from Oldenburg, consul at Brunswick; and Francis J. Klauser of Ohio, born in Württemberg, consul at Amsterdam.[10]

Lincoln gave federal jobs, in addition to consular and diplomatic posts, to German American leaders as well. Particularly prominent was Reinhold Solger, born in Stettin and a literary figure, whom Lincoln made assistant registrar of the US Treasury, a job specifically created for him by Congress. When it came to distributing federal patronage, Lincoln remembered full well those citizens of German birth who had aided in the creation and success of his Republican Party.

Diplomatic appointments, though, were a touchy subject, and Carl Schurz was not the only one of Lincoln's closest German friends who found himself disappointed. "Before the 4th of March it was currently reported, that you would confer the [minister] to Berlin mission on me," wrote Gustave Koerner to Lincoln, "The entire Press, American & German mentioned the appointment as almost a positive fact. It got into the German Papers in Europe. I received letters from here and from Germany of congratulation." Lincoln had appointed another old Illinois friend, Norman Judd, to this ministerial position, and the entire situation mortified Koerner. Judd's appointment was a grave disappointment to the Germans, who had expected Lincoln to appoint someone who spoke their native language, Koerner maintained. "I candidly confess, however," he continued, "that as the thing happened, under the peculiar attitude in which I had been placed, I felt deeply affected. It certainly disappointed all my friends. . . . As I know the language . . . in addition to French, the diplomatic language of the world, as I know the history of the people, their manners, their laws, and by my vast acquaintance with men now high in office, [I] could have done something just at this [secession] crisis to retain for our country their sympathy, I considered myself as being in any mission in Germany more useful, than perhaps many others who aspired to the respective places."

Koerner felt betrayed by Lincoln for his failure to offer him a diplomatic position to a German-speaking nation. Further, there seemed to be a growing rivalry between Koerner and Carl Schurz for Lincoln's attention. Koerner appeared particularly chagrined by the initial appointment of Schurz to the Madrid embassy. "I am of your age. Have worked very hard in my profession," Koerner wrote to Lincoln. "Young active Germans, of merits, undoubtedly, but not half so well known to the Germans of the United States, and who had great prospects before them at home in the sphere, in which they excel, were favored in the missions. I stood disgraced in the eyes of others, not in my own. I had done nothing to forfeit your friendship and the regard you have always shown me. I think my quiet and unobtrusive manner has not lowered me in your estimation. I know I could not have pressed my claims on your attention for the world." When Koerner did not receive the diplomatic position that he sought, he concluded that he was "being considered every where as neglected & orphaned by your administration."[11]

Lincoln, however, had other plans for Koerner and soon appointed him to the rank of colonel and aide-de-camp to General John C. Frémont's staff in Missouri, where his old German friend soon found himself embroiled in an ethnic and military controversy. German troops were enraged by what they regarded as insulting treatment of one of their own, General Franz Sigel. Since the Battle of Cedar

Mountain in August 1862, Sigel had come under heavy criticism from his military and political superiors, who doubted his ability. Sigel had been neither well received nor respected by the West Pointers, who resented a major generalship in the East being assigned to a German. Not part of their clique, Sigel was treated as an outsider by the West Pointers, not only because he was German but because he was a political appointment as well. His haughty and gruff manner seemed to invite criticism and exacerbated an already bitter feeling toward him. General Henry Halleck, general in chief of all Union armies, called him a "damned coward," an opinion not shared by others, and complained that Sigel's corps "comprised some of the best fighting men that we have [although] it wouldn't do much under Sigel." His and Secretary of War Edwin Stanton's treatment of Sigel enraged the Germans in the army as well as the German press.

The apparent mistreatment of Sigel also did not go unnoticed by non-Germans. Future president James Garfield was disgusted by Halleck's and Stanton's lack of respect for Sigel. Garfield was critical of Halleck's "cold as a stone personality" and the fact that he cared "not a penny for the work, only as a professional performance." "There is that glorious Sigel," he wrote, "stripped down to 7,000 men and placed under an inferior, both in rank and ability. His men have been sent away to swell McClellan's already overgrown army." "Sigel could," Garfield concluded, "if he had the force, strike a fatal blow upon the Rebel's rear and flank," but that was "under the quasi ban of West Point. If the Republic goes down in blood and ruin, let its obituary be written then 'Died of West Point.'" The feeling was widespread that Sigel had been the object of petty and prejudicial retaliation, and as one observer recalled, "Stanton was an irritating pettifogger . . . [he] and Halleck hated foreigners. . . . As for Sigel he is so ill-treated that they say he will be obliged to resign. . . . We are under infidel rule."[12]

Sigel contemplated resignation, and popular protests sprung up on his behalf. The thought of one of their favorite generals being threatened with removal mobilized the Germans' support and participation. General Carl Schurz, returning from his diplomatic post in Spain, was equally disturbed by the Sigel affair and expressed his misgivings to Lincoln about the unfair treatment of Sigel. Lincoln, however, was keenly aware of the political importance of the Germans, and his view of foreigners was different from Halleck's and Stanton's. When resolutions in support of Sigel arrived from a meeting of five thousand Germans held at Cooper Institute in New York, Lincoln assured the German American leaders that he would inquire into the matter. He told them that Sigel would be placed at the top of his list in case a vacancy opened for major general and then ordered newly commissioned Koerner to investigate the Sigel case.

To quiet the roiling waters, Lincoln wrote to General Henry Halleck and asked Koerner to deliver it.[13] "The Germans are true and patriotic, and so far as they have got cross in Missouri it is upon mistake and misunderstanding," Lincoln lectured Halleck. "Without a knowledge of its contents Governor Koerner, of Illinois, will hand you this letter. He is an educated and talented German gentleman, as true a man as lives. With his assistance you can set everything right with the Germans. . . . My clear judgment is that, with reference to the German element in your command, you should have Governor Koerner with you; and if agreeable to you and him, I will make him a brigadier-general, so that he can afford to so give his time. He does not wish to command in the field, though he has more knowledge than many who do. If he goes into the place he will simply be an efficient, zealous, and unselfish assistant to you."[14] Halleck ignored Lincoln's suggestion and replied to the president, "The difficulty with the Germans results from . . . 1st the want of pay, the Pay Dept. here being out of funds . . . 2d They are continually tampered with by designing politicians. . . . A part of the scheme is the story about the ill-treatment of Genl. Sigel. . . . All these difficulties are being satisfactorily arranged. A firm and decided course will end them forever. Being a German myself by descent, I know something of the German character, and I am confident that in a few weeks, if the Govt does not interfere, I can reduce these disaffected elements to order & discipline." In the end the military promotion of Koerner became moot when Lincoln changed course and appointed him to replace Schurz as minister to Spain, where he served in that role until August 1864.[15]

Koerner might not have been militarily promoted, but Sigel was. Before leaving for Spain, Koerner had harsh words for Halleck in a letter to Lincoln: "If he [Halleck] had known the temper of the Germans just at this time smarting under some real and imaginary wrongs . . . if he had known the great admiration in which Sigel is held . . . [he] would never have made [his] unfortunate move in supplying his place . . . by Gen. Curtis . . . the appointment of Genl. Sigel as a Major General would give [the Germans] general and unbounded satisfaction, even if he should be appointed on the Potomac." Sigel was nominated major general on March 3 and confirmed by the Senate eighteen days later. Wisely, Lincoln maintained that he had been impressed by Sigel's brave performance at the Battle of Pea Ridge and had promoted Sigel because of his strategy and courage. Sigel had earned his promotion on the field, Lincoln insisted, and not through politics. Lincoln's insistence notwithstanding, this whole episode demonstrated yet again the significance of the Germans to Lincoln.[16]

Whatever problems Lincoln may have had with the Germans early in the war, they were soon exacerbated by General John C. Frémont's arrogance and incompetence. Surrounded by primarily German staff officers, Frémont, commanding the Department of the West headquartered in St. Louis, issued an order on August 30, 1861, that declared martial law in Missouri, threatened to court-martial and shoot citizens found in possession of firearms, and ordered the confiscation of property and the freeing of slaves of active enemies of the Union. It was the last stipulation that made Frémont a hero of the antislavery German element. Thanks to Frémont, what had begun as a campaign by German immigrants to save the state of Missouri for the Union had now turned into a revolution to overturn the system of labor in a state hanging by a tenuous thread in the Union. While Lincoln was assuring the border states of Kentucky, Maryland, and Missouri that he was not waging war on slavery, Frémont, the Germans' champion, had taken unilateral steps to free the slaves in Missouri.

Writing to Frémont, Lincoln took issue with most of the general's proclamation and stated, "There is great danger [that] the liberating slaves of traitorous owners, will alarm our Southern Union friends, and turn them against us—perhaps ruin our rather fair prospect for Kentucky." Lincoln asked Frémont to modify his proclamation, believing that keeping Kentucky in the Union was one of the keys to winning the war. Frémont proved obstinate, and after two turbulent months of trying to deal with his defiant general, the president removed him from his command on October 24, 1861.

Frémont instantly became a martyr to the Germans and other antislavery advocates. The St. Louis German community was outraged by what they saw as a betrayal by Lincoln of their antislavery beliefs, the first principle of the Republican Party. Some Germans even vowed to dedicate themselves to Lincoln's reelection defeat in 1864. The Germans who did so, however, were the ones who ultimately lost. By allying themselves with the emancipationist but militarily incompetent General Frémont, these Germans antagonized many of the state's native-born and Irish Unionists, and they consequently lost all of their political capital by being associated with the general's dictatorial actions. Already at the liberal end of the state's political spectrum, they became even more marginalized and less politically viable, as their defense of the unpopular Frémont put them at odds even with Lincoln.[17]

Lincoln personally knew German immigrants, had powerful German friends, and obviously gave favors to Germans, including Carl Schurz, Gustave Koerner, and Franz Sigel.[18] Although Lincoln spoke of Germans often, he rarely spoke or wrote of Irish immigrants, and when he did, it was not usually in flattering terms. Lincoln warned the Republicans to watch for cheating by the Irish in Chicago and elsewhere during the 1858 senatorial election and again during his run for the presidency two years later. These warnings would seem to indicate his distrust of Irish immigrants, though it also may be interpreted as his fear of their growing political power within the rival Democratic Party. Irish immigrants were usually supportive of the Southern slave owners and opposed to any policies that would result in the emancipation of slaves.

Both before and during the 1860 campaign, Lincoln was questioned several times about his attitude toward the Irish. One Illinois resident wrote to Lincoln, asking if he was "against the people who profess the Roman Catholic Church. We have a large number of Irish men here; many of them are dissatisfied of the democratic pretension and they are willing to vote for the Republican candidate for the presidency if they did positively know the true opinions of Hon. Abraham Lincoln." Another wrote, "There are in our country over 100 Catholic Irish votes as yet they are not set. But we cannot get them. The stronghold of Catholicism is in the Slave states. Despotism suits the spirit of Catholicism better than freedom. [Roger] Taney is a Catholic, and the Southern 'State Equality' doctrine, as elucidated by the 'Dred Scott' dictum, they will be ready to endorse. They like also to be on the side of the Powers that be. Again the rank and file vote according to the crook of the Priest's finger. There is a large Catholic vote in this state and it will go as a unit. . . . Cannot a spring be touched somewhere that will commit the priests[?]" A New York City woman informed Lincoln that the city was "largely democratic in consequence of the prevailing prejudice among the ignorant class of Irish & German, that the Republican Party are opposed to giving patronage to foreigners—Now if this can be removed by judicious appointments to our city thousands can be won over to the Republican party." Uncharacteristically, Lincoln did not respond to any of these challenges.[19]

Lincoln had little success with the Irish, dating back to the founding of the Republican Party. The *Boston Pilot* speculated that it was inconceivable that the Irish would support the "Black Republicans," who were "hostile to the Constitution and engaged in spreading flames of discord and war." The editor of the *Irish News* damned the Republican acceptance of the Know Nothings and predicted, "The foreign [Irish] vote . . . will preserve the Union." During the first Republican campaign in 1856, the Irish were reminded that it was the Democrats who had defended them against nativists and protected them from black labor competition, that Frémont was the "English nominee," and that the Republicans were "the Puritanical party."[20]

By the time Lincoln ran for president, the Irish were as dubious about his qualifications as millions of other Americans. The *Boston Pilot* sarcastically commented, "[Some] very good men have made their marks, Lincoln made his—with an axe." Although the

Republican Party organized a few "Wide Awake" clubs, there were few Irish Republicans. Unlike the Germans, the vast numbers of Irish remained within the Democratic Party and in 1860 cast their ballots for Stephen Douglas. The *Irish News* was certain that Lincoln could be easily defeated and that William Seward would have made a stronger candidate. Indeed, Irish leaders launched such a stream of invectives against Lincoln and his party that Horace Greeley warned them in an editorial that while the Republican Party welcomed "friendly counsel," it would not accept "dictation." "He who votes in our election as an Irishman or German," Greeley admonished, "has no moral right to vote at all."[21]

Although Lincoln and the Republican Party recognized their obligation to the German voters, many of whom had shifted in their loyalties from the Democrats to the Republicans in 1860, Lincoln's party as yet owed little to the Irish. In truth, the Irish in New York City saw Lincoln's election as an abject disaster. A great "Union meeting" at Cooper Institute on January 28, 1861, became a virtual mockery of Unionist sentiment. The meeting grew out of an appeal to all parties who were *against* Lincoln. James T. Brady, the principal speaker, was a prominent "responsible" Irishman, an attorney and future judge. Brady, declaring that he did not believe in coercion, urged the South to be patient and generous while the North sorted out its problems. Lincoln had strong opposition in the Irish population even as he prepared to assume the burdens of office. That fact notwithstanding, it was not long before the Irish American press complained that the Irish were being ignored by the new administration in matters of commissions in the Union army and in political patronage.[22]

Although Lincoln moved cautiously and much too slowly for many of his party when it came to the emancipation of slaves, the Irish soon became critical of him for moving too fast. When John C. Frémont issued his proclamation in 1861 freeing the slaves in his military district of Missouri, the *Pilot* branded it a high-handed violation of the constitution and defiance of the national government. Other Irish newspapers joined in the swelling chorus of criticism of Lincoln and his administration. The *New York Metropolitan Record* asserted that the Irish had been cheated by the government, which had asked them to serve as Irishmen and now "made [them] subservient to the emancipation of the negro." The Irish papers strongly opposed Lincoln's proposal to end slavery in the border states and hammered away at Lincoln's "dictatorship" and any policy that smacked of emancipation of Southern slaves. John Mullaly, editor of the *Metropolitan Record*, demanded the impeachment of Lincoln to end the "march of despotism" and argued for an immediate armistice, to be followed by a peace convention that would recognize the sovereignty of the Southern states. Mullaly claimed that his anti-Lincoln editorials won him three thousand new subscribers in two months and soon published them in a book that began with a parody of Alfred, Lord Tennyson: "Abraham Lincoln, we bow the knee, Republican King; Yankees and Yorkers, and Quakers are we, The rightful heirs of the men once free, But all of us slaves in our worship of thee, Republican King."[23]

Like the Germans, the Irish demanded that Lincoln recognize their countrymen in the military. They even demanded separate Hibernian units in the Union army and also requested an entire Irish division. When this was refused, they felt sorely aggrieved, and the Irish press echoed their feeling in visceral anti-Lincoln language. The Irish resented it when James Shields, one of Lincoln's old political rivals from Illinois, was not made a major general, and they pointed out that there were only two Irish brigadiers. The *Boston Pilot* criticized Lincoln for failure to appoint Irishmen to important jobs in government, and Archbishop John Hughes, in a letter to William Seward, urged that Colonel Michael Corcoran of the Irish brigade be made a brigadier because Hughes had "discovered symptoms of wounded feelings among his countrymen."[24]

Ever the pragmatic politician, Lincoln called on the archbishop to request advice on Catholic chaplains during the Civil War. He also made Hughes an emissary to Europe, sending him to the Vatican, England, and France in 1861 and 1862 to urge nonintervention in the war. "Having formed the Archbishop's acquaintance in the earliest days of our country's present troubles," Lincoln wrote, "his counsel and advice were gladly sought and continually received by the Government on those points which his position enabled him better than others to consider. At a conjuncture of deep interest to the country, the Archbishop associated with others, went abroad, and did the nation a service there with all the loyalty, fidelity, and practical wisdom which on so many other occasions illustrated his great ability for administration." Hughes had fought anti-Catholic and nativist intolerance for many years, and Lincoln's reliance on him clearly indicated that the president was not inhibited by the prejudice of which he was accused by many of Hughes's fellow countrymen.[25]

Still, there was much jealousy between the Germans and the Irish during the Civil War. Both furnished many soldiers, but each thought the other was favored by Lincoln. The *Metropolitan Record* criticized Lincoln for making Carl Schurz "a general before he was fit to be a citizen" and for giving Major General Franz Sigel his pay for "doing nothing." The Irish believed that General Patrick H. Kelly had been removed from command in western Virginia simply to create a command position for Sigel, and they were utterly disgusted when the rumor spread that the president was to send his eldest son, Robert, to Europe "to learn High Dutch."[26]

For the most part, the Irish steadfastly remained Democratic in their party affiliation and unlike the Germans, who had a change of political heart, never warmed up to Lincoln. Indicative of this was a letter that Christopher Byrne, an Irishman in the Union army, wrote home to his brother in Ireland. "You are already aware," Byrne said, "that there was two great parties in this country that was entirely opposed to each other, one a proslavery party, the other abolition party. The latter party was always a meddling party, not content to attend to their own business without interfering with their neighbors. This abolition party are a set of discontented Fanatics who would rather rule in hell than to serve in heaven. When they are not interfering with the rights of foreignors [*sic*] or proscribing Religious Denominations, they are Speech making in favor of abolition. . . . The republican, or abolition party, as I may call it . . . elected their president which has so far proved fatal to the country." Byrne's letter was written in 1863, after Lincoln's Emancipation Proclamation went into effect, thereby making the abolition of slavery one of the Union's new war objectives.[27]

The Irish were particularly incensed by Lincoln's proclamation. Especially in New York, Irish immigrants heard a steady stream of invective from their leaders, such as Congressman Michael Walsh, an angry voice for the Irish who apparently had quite a flair for stump speaking. "Slangy, raucous, and sarcastic, with a brassy face and cool, undaunted manner, he would drawl out rambling speeches which convulsed his audiences with their wit and ridicule," one observer noted. Walsh never hesitated to excite and agitate fellow countrymen. "The great and fruitful source of crime and misery on earth is the inequality of society," he shouted out, "the abject dependence of honest willing industry upon idle and dishonest capitalists. [Republican] Demagogues will tell you that you are free men. They lie; you are slaves. No man, devoid of all other means of support but that which his own labor affords him, can be a freeman, under the present state of society." And on another occasion Walsh drove home his point by proclaiming, "What have we gained by the numberless political victories we have achieved? Nothing but a change of masters!"

The Irish did indeed believe that freed slaves would present a threat to their livelihood and security in American society. While most of the North moved toward an antislavery position, the Irish moved in the opposite direction. Despite famed politician Daniel O'Connell's urgings from Ireland and a papal bull against the slave trade, the Irish in the North hardened their position against Lincoln and abolition. Fearful of losing whatever economic advantage they might hold, New York's Irish heard Walsh conclude one of his fiery anti-Lincoln speeches by saying, "The only difference between the Negro slave of the South and the [Irish] white wage slave of the North is that one has a master without asking him, and the other has to beg for the privilege of becoming a slave. The one is the slave of an individual; the other is the slave of an inexorable class. It is very well for gentlemen . . . to clamor about the wrongs and outrages of southern slaves but, sir, even in New York, during the last year there have been over thirteen hundred people deprived of their liberty without any show or color of offense, but because they were poor, and too honest to commit crimes."[28]

Michael Walsh notwithstanding, the Irish rallied with enthusiasm to Lincoln's call for volunteer troops after the firing on Fort Sumter. It has been estimated that fifty-one thousand of the troops who served the Union army from New York State were born in Ireland. And by the fall of 1861 several regiments were joined together to create the Irish Brigade, under the command of General Thomas Meagher, a hero of the Irish Revolution in 1848. As William L. D. O'Grady reported, one of Meagher's junior officers, First Lieutenant R. H. Bermingham of the 69th New York, later recorded that when Lincoln visited the army at Harrison's Landing on the James River in Virginia, he was so moved by the Irish Brigade's sacrifices in General George McClellan's Peninsula Campaign that the president lifted the corner of a green regimental flag, kissed it, and exclaimed, "God bless the Irish Flag." O'Grady concluded, "Lincoln was not gushy, but the roll of the brick and ball muskets of the brigade at Fair Oaks and their conduct on the seven days' 'change of base' were matters of recent occurrence and official commendation."[29]

Nevertheless, under the 1863 conscription law, the Irish believed that they bore a disproportionate burden of the new draft. As a result of the massive losses that the Union had sustained during the first two years of the war, coupled with decreased enlistments due to low morale, President Lincoln had signed the Enrollment Act into law on March 3, 1863. The act, titled in full "An act for enrolling and calling out the National Forces and for other purposes," required all able-bodied men between the ages of twenty and forty-five to register for possible military service, and a lottery determined the order in which men were called up. The names of conscripts would subsequently be printed by the draft office and in the newspapers. The act contained a provision that men who could afford to pay a commutation fee of $300, or who could arrange for a substitute, could buy their way out of the service. The bulk of the Irish, though, were laboring men who could not afford the $300.

The first drawing of names in New York City, on Saturday, July 11, produced a list of twelve hundred men, the majority of whom were Irish. This announcement came with special impact after two years of fighting in which the Irish regiments had suffered heavy losses. There was widespread anger following Lincoln's Emancipation Proclamation on January 1, 1863, for it seemed to the Irish, and others, that a war begun to save the Union had turned into a war to free the slaves. The tension between Irish and African Americans in New York City had been growing for three months, since African American "scabs" had been used in April 1863 to break a bitter dock strike led by Irish longshoremen. On Monday morning following the first draft list of inductees, Irish workingmen stayed away from their jobs and began to gather in angry crowds outside the draft centers and on vacant lots on the East Side near Central Park. When the police, great numbers of whom were Irish, attempted under the leadership of Superintendent John Kennedy to disperse the crowds, they turned and fought. Kennedy was badly beaten, and the rioting lasted for four days. The Irish mobs went from place to place, attacking the armory on Lexington Avenue and various private houses. The main object of Irish wrath was African Americans. The Colored Orphan Asylum was burned; hapless individual African Americans who were seen on the streets were beaten and several were hanged. "It was a classic example," one observer wrote, "of the poor in their misery by venting their fury on other poor who were even worse off."

Archbishop John Hughes, the revered leader of the Irish community, used his influence in an attempt to calm down his countrymen. Addressing a great crowd from the balcony of his residence on the fourth day of rioting, the archbishop said, "If you are Irishmen—for your enemies say the rioters are Irishmen—I am also an Irishman, but not a rioter. If you are Catholic, as they have reported—then I am a Catholic too. I know that under the misguidance of real or imaginary evils, people will sometimes get uneasy . . . ; but I think with the poet that it is better to bear out slight inconveniences than to rush to evils that we have not yet witnessed. . . . When these so-called riots are over, and the blame is justly laid on the Irish Catholics, I wish you to tell me in what country I could claim to be born?"[30]

Eventually Lincoln ordered troops from the Army of the Potomac, still recovering from the bloodying it had taken at Gettysburg, to march to New York City and restore order. Moreover, the police, naval personnel, and a company from West Point also came to quell the disturbance. More than a hundred people were killed in what became known as the New York City draft riots. In spite of the chaos, however, martial law was never enacted in the city, and despite many of the accusations leveled against him, Lincoln left the restoration of the city's order in the hands of local politicians.

Lincoln was besieged with requests to delay or suspend the draft in one state or another throughout the war. But after the New York City riot, the Democratic governor of New York, Horatio Seymour, who thought the draft to be unconstitutional in the first place, argued that it should be suspended until the Supreme Court weighed in on its constitutionality. Lincoln refused, though he wrote to Seymour, "I do not object to abide a decision of the United States Supreme Court, or of the judges thereof, on the constitutionality of the draft law. In fact, I should be willing to facilitate the obtaining of it; but I cannot consent to lose the *time* while it is being obtained." He then took pains to compare the Union draft law with that of the Confederacy. "We are contending with an enemy who, as I understand, drives every able bodied man he can reach, into his ranks, very much like a butcher drives bullocks into a slaughter-open. No time is wasted, no argument is used."[31]

Lincoln agreed to reduce some quotas that apparently fell heavily on Irish wards and to have a commission investigate inequities in New York's quotas. He also sent General John A. Dix, a New York Democrat, to command Union troops in the state. But the draft resumed without incident on August 19. Even though more than a hundred people had died, Lincoln did not change the Enrollment Act. Through various means, most of the Irishmen, as well as some Germans and Jews, opposed to fighting in the Union army were exempted; the New York Board of Supervisors funded the replacement of many drafted working-class men. In the end Lincoln was not particularly pressured by events in New York to change his policy.

But the relationship between Lincoln and the Irish had been poisoned even more. The *New York Herald* described the draft riots as "a popular outbreak inspired by a burning sense of wrong," and the *New York World* commented that apparently "poor men refused to be forced into a war" that was mismanaged and perverted to partisan purposes. Even Bishop Hughes could not masquerade his criticism of Lincoln in a letter he sent to his friend, Secretary of State William Seward. The riot was caused, wrote Hughes, by the Lincoln administration seeking "to make black labor equal to white labor . . . with the difference being that black labor shall have local patronage over the toil of the white man."[32]

Lincoln was castigated for being anti-Irish and anti-Catholic and for refusing to accept them as he did other immigrant groups, such as the Germans and Jews. The heart of the matter, however, was the Irish attitude toward slavery in the South. If Lincoln had problems with the Irish, in all likelihood the road began there. For most of Lincoln's life, he was a strong proponent of the free labor and free soil philosophy. After all, he need not look any farther than himself to see what hard work, diligence, and perseverance could accomplish. Because the United States had so much land and so much economic opportunity, proponents of the free labor theory such as Lincoln often concluded that no one need remain poor. Laborers could strive to become free landholders, and an entire "inferior" class—in the words of Senator James Henry Hammond of South Carolina, a "mud sill" class of perpetually poor and economically enslaved workers—could rise to respectability.

"The prudent, penniless beginner in the world, labors for wages awhile, saves a surplus with which to buy tools or land, for himself; then labors on his own account another while, and at great length hires another new beginner to help him," Lincoln said in a speech. "This say its advocates, is free labor—the just and generous, and prosperous system, which opens the way for all—gives hope to all, and energy, and progress, and improvement of condition to all." As a self-made man who had escaped poverty and the condition of his father, Lincoln believed that all men were capable of rising socially and economically. "If any continue through life in the condition of the hired laborer," Lincoln asserted, "it is not the fault of the system, but either because of a dependent nature which prefers it, or improvidence, folly or singular misfortune."[33] First as a Whig, then later as a Republican, Lincoln espoused this belief and seldom wavered from it. The free soil, free labor platform of the Republicans fit Lincoln very comfortably.

Yet many of Lincoln's fellow Republicans harbored some strong nativist tendencies and visceral anti-Catholic feelings and held the Irish in very low regard. They accepted the contemporary stereotypes of Irish as lazy, shiftless, and willingly poor. Many cartoons of the day depicted the Irish as appropriate "mud sill" dwellers, unlike their counterpart immigrant group, the Germans. To listen to the speeches of Michael Walsh, the Irish were forced into the most menial urban jobs, and few of them were able to advance according to the free labor, free land theory of Lincoln and the Republicans. Many of the Republicans, then, believed that the Irish remained "wage slaves" through their own fault and were not industrious enough to rise out of poverty. Unfair though it may be, in the minds of many Republicans, the Irish were condemned to a life of impoverishment. The Germans, however, were fierce free soil advocates and had a support system based on a network of economic, political, and social organizations. They were vehemently antislavery as well. They had Lincoln's respect, and he had, for the most part, their votes.

If one takes Lincoln at his word, it is entirely possible that he did not have much understanding of the immigrant Irish, except for their willingness to fight hard for the Union army. Although he had visited New York City and New England, Lincoln had not seen the congested mill towns of the East or the Irish slums of New York City. He was a product of a political climate that favored rural environs over urban, and he saw opportunity in terms of one's ability to own property. In short, the urban Irish represented a challenge to Lincoln's long-held economic philosophy, and those beliefs might have clouded his opinion of the Irish as an immigrant group.

Lincoln's often confusing religious beliefs might have affected his relationship with the Irish as well as the Jews. It is doubtful that he met many Catholics or Jews while growing up. In all likelihood, Lincoln probably had not met a Jew before he met fellow Illinois lawyer Abraham Jonas at age thirty. Jonas soon became one of Lincoln's enthusiastic political supporters and a man that Lincoln would refer to as one of his "most valued friends."[34] Soon afterward, Lincoln made the acquaintance of a number of Jews as friends, associates, and colleagues, and as he did with the Germans, he won them over and gained their support. That notwithstanding, Lincoln's world was one where he could refer to Americans as a "Christian people" in an order for the military observance of the Sabbath on November 15, 1862. "The importance for man and beast of the prescribed weekly rest, the sacred rights of Christian soldiers, a becoming deference to the best sentiment of a Christian people, and a due regard for the Divine will," Lincoln wrote, "demand that Sunday labor in the Army and Navy be reduced to the measure of strict necessity. . . . The first General Order issued by the Father of his Country after the Declaration of Independence, indicates the spirit in which our institutions were founded and should ever be defended: '*The General hopes and trusts that every officer and man will endeavor to live and act as becomes a Christian solider defending the dearest rights and liberties of his country.*'"[35] Once again Lincoln's inexperience with an urban immigrant group might have inadvertently clouded his recognition that the Jews could conceivably be insulted by their exclusion from his speech.

And indeed they were. The law regarding military chaplains required that they be "regular ordained ministers of some Christian denomination." This stipulation led Secretary of War Simon Cameron to reject Arnold Fischel's application for appointment as chaplain of the Cameron Dragoons of New York, a district heavily populated by Jewish residents. Frustrated, Jewish leaders went public. They published editorials in Jewish periodicals, solicited liberal newspapers to support them, and sent a delegation to the White House. There Fischel begged Lincoln to recognize "the principle of religious liberty . . . the constitutional rights of the Jewish community, and the welfare of the Jewish volunteers" who were dying in battle without access to spiritual support. Convinced and chagrined, Lincoln wrote to Fischel, "My dear Sir: I find that there are several particulars in which the present law in regard to Chaplains is supposed to be deficient, all of which I now design presenting to the appropriate Committee of Congress. I shall try to have a new law broad enough to cover what is desired by you on behalf of the Israelites." Three months later, on March 12, 1862, Lincoln signed such a bill into law. The old statute was duly amended to include all "regularly ordained ministers of some denomination." The word "Christian" was expunged. And shortly thereafter Lincoln named Rabbi Jacob Frankel of Philadelphia as the first Jewish chaplain in American history. The Jews, under Lincoln, had reversed four score years of institutional discrimination within the army.[36]

Isachar Zacharie, a chiropodist who operated on Lincoln's feet in 1862, gained the president's confidence enough to be sent twice on mysterious missions to New Orleans, which had a large and influential Jewish community. The *New York Herald* had a field day with Zacharie's relationship with the president: "The President has been greatly blamed for not resisting the demands of the radicals; but how could the President put his foot down firmly when he was troubled with corns? . . . It would seem therefore, that all our past troubles have originated not so much with the head as with the feet of the nation. Dr. Zacharie has shown us precisely where the shoe pinches." Lincoln enjoyed this humor a great deal and read press like this often to his friends. And it is entirely possible that the editorial satirists were at least partially responsible for the cordial relationship that developed between the president and his foot doctor.[37]

Zacharie was to be "a means of access to his countrymen, who are quite numerous in some of the localities you will probably visit," Lincoln stated. Such a mission was not without peril. Lincoln's adversaries reflected the prevalent prejudice of the day, labeling Zacharie "the lowest and vulgarest form of Jew Peddlar," while saying of Lincoln, "It is enough to condemn Mr. Lincoln that he can make a friend of such an odious creature." To his credit, Lincoln was not swayed by such bigotry. After the Battle of Gettysburg and the fall of Vicksburg, Lincoln sent Zacharie to Richmond on another mysterious mission, to meet with Confederate leaders, perhaps about a peace plan. Lincoln's faith in the Jewish surgeon was reciprocated. Zacharie became fiercely loyal to Lincoln and actively campaigned among the Jewish community for his reelection in 1864. "The Isrelites [*sic*] with but few exceptions, they will vote for you," Zacharie wrote to Lincoln. "I understand them well and have taken the precaution to see that they do as they have promised. I have secured good and trustworthy men to attend to them on Election Day. My men have been all the week seeing that their major masses are properly registered—so that all will be right [in November]."[38]

But Zacharie's efforts created jealously within the Jewish community. Some Jews took issue with Zacharie's claim that he could deliver the Jewish vote to Lincoln and even with the idea that there was such a thing as a monolithic Jewish vote. "There is no 'Jewish vote,'" the *Jewish Messenger* editor Meyer Isaacs wrote angrily to Lincoln, "and if there were it could not be bought. Nobody is authorized to speak for our co-religionists on political questions." This political and religious infighting threatened to erupt into a political minicrisis for Lincoln until he ordered one of his secretaries, John Hay, to write to the Jewish leaders and reassure them. "No pledge of the Jewish vote was made by these gentlemen," Hay told Isaacs, "and no inducements or promises were extended to them by the President. They claimed no such authority and received no such response as you seem to suppose—The President deems this statement due to you."[39]

An intensely ambitious individual, Zacharie rubbed many of Lincoln's advisors the wrong way. Lincoln, though, liked Zacharie, and what he saw beneath the chiropodist's glibness and aggressiveness struck the president as sound enough to welcome him to Washington whenever he visited, send him to New Orleans and Richmond to work out policy, and listen to his analysis of political developments, while all the time he remained an unknown, unimportant foreigner to many in Lincoln's cabinet. Whatever Zacharie's motives were for winning Lincoln's favor, Lincoln liked him well enough to discuss matters of important state policy with him and while away hours of despondency in his company.[40]

The greatest test of Lincoln's tolerance of immigrant Jews was yet to come: the notorious anti-Semitic Order No. 11, issued by General Ulysses Grant. Convinced that Jews were infiltrating his encampments and speculating, profiteering, and conducting contraband trade, Grant was determined to root them out. In July 1862 Grant began issuing orders to his officers to deny Jews permits and to pay special attention to them. "No Jews are to be permitted to travel on the Rail Road southward from any point," he wrote. "They are such an intolerable nuisance, that the department must be purged of them." "My policy,"

Grant insisted, "is to exclude them as far as practicable." Grant's General Order No. 11 on July 17 stated in part, "The Jews, as a class violating every regulation of trade . . . are hereby expelled from the department territory under Grant's military control in the Ohio and Mississippi Valleys within 24 hours. . . . Post commanders will see that all of this class of people be . . . required to leave, and any one returning after such notification will be arrested and held in confinement."[41]

The Jews were outraged, and Lincoln heard about it loudly from various quarters. A Jewish captain named Philip Trounstine promptly resigned his commission, complaining of "taunts and malice." Not long thereafter, Jewish residents of Paducah, Kentucky, were expelled along with their wives and children, prompting a protest to Lincoln against the "outrageous treatment of Jewish families of this town as outlaws before the whole world." Respected Northern rabbis unleashed a firestorm of criticism from the pulpit and the press.

Grant's order, outside of believing that the general was simply anti-Semitic, can only be understood against the background of the confusion, corruption, inefficiency, and heated feelings involved in the contraband trade of the border states. The area had become an epicenter of all types of illegal trading in cotton, machinery, medical supplies, and food. And while it is probably true that some Jews were engaged in the illicit business dealings of the area, Grant's motivation for his condemnation of Jews as a class was without doubt discriminatory and prejudicial.

In a letter to Grant on January 21, 1863, General Henry Halleck revoked Grant's order by writing, "It may be proper to give you some explanation of the revocation of your order expelling all Jews from your department. The President has no objection to your expelling traitors and Jew peddlers, which, I suppose, was the object of your order; but, as it in terms proscribed an entire religious class, some of whom are fighting in our ranks, the President deemed it necessary to revoke it."[42]

Grant's anti-Jewish insensitivity caused some embarrassment for Lincoln. But it easily could have been forgiven by the Christian majority of 1862. Lincoln might have ignored the outcry for fear of humiliating or annoying one of his most valuable military assets, but to his credit, he did not excuse or cover up for Grant. On one of the rare occasions in which he overruled his prize general, Lincoln made sure that General Order No. 11 was rescinded. In short, he came to the rescue of the Jews. Lincoln "had expressed an interest in seeing justice done to the Jews," one observer wrote, "and was willing to take upon himself the responsibility for the necessary action. He understood of democratic equality enough to know that no group could be deprived of its rights without endangering the whole structure of democracy." When Rabbi Isaac Mayer Wise of Cincinnati came to the White House to protest Grant's order, the president spoke to him in no uncertain terms. Wise recalled, "The President fully convinced us that he knew of no distinction between Jews and Gentiles and that he feels none against any nationality and especially against Israelites," and "by no means will [he] allow that a citizen in any wise be wronged on account of his place of birth or religious confession." "To condemn a class," Wise quoted Lincoln, "is, to say the least, to wrong the good with the bad. I do not like to hear a class or nationality condemned on account of a few sinners."[43]

At about the same time, Lincoln made the acquaintance of a rather strange and visionary Jewish man by the name of Henry Wentworth Monk. Monk had come to Washington to meet with Lincoln to urge upon the president a plan to end the war. Lincoln was not seriously disposed to entertain any of Monk's proposals, so Monk went on to discuss one of his pet projects: the restoration of European Jewry to Palestine. Lincoln agreed that the vision Monk had of a Jewish state in Palestine was worthy of consideration but maintained that the United States was in no position to take a leading role in international affairs until it had set its own house in order and reunited the two warring sections. "I myself have a high regard for the Jews," Lincoln told Monk. "My chiropodist is a Jew, and he has so many times 'put me upon my feet' that I would have no objection to giving his countrymen 'a leg up,'" the president punned.[44] This passing reference to Zacharie was the only other known opinion that Lincoln ever registered in regard to the Jews, beyond the general comments he made to Isaac Mayer Wise and his friends about Grant's order and to Arnold Fischel concerning the chaplaincy clause. In those two cases Lincoln had expressed an interest in seeing justice done to the Jews and was willing to take the responsibility of necessary action. Lincoln's experiences with Jewish individuals from his Illinois years on undoubtedly helped him realize that Jews, like all the other immigrants he encountered, were no different from other human beings, despite the widespread prejudices against them.

With this attitude in mind, in some ways Lincoln staked the entire conduct of the war on the shoulders of an immigrant. During the hot and desperate summer of 1862 Major General Henry Halleck, who had become general in chief of the Union armies, was consumed with questions about the treatment of the Confederates. Soon discovering that the army had no laws or regulations to govern its contacts with the bands of Confederate guerrilla forces in the field, Halleck, a lawyer by trade, found this absence of guidance to be frustrating. Union troops were increasingly encountering an array of rebel forces, some uniformed and others not. "The rebel authorities claim the right to send men, in the garb of peaceful citizens, to waylay and attack our troops, to burn bridges and houses, and to destroy property and persons within our lines," Halleck wrote. "They demand that such persons be treated as ordinary belligerents, and that when captured they have extended to them the same rights as other prisoners of war; they also threaten that if such persons be punished as marauders and spies they will retaliate by executing our prisoners of war in their possession. I particularly request your views on these questions." The person to whom Halleck addressed his question was a Prussian immigrant, Professor Francis Lieber of Columbia College (now the University of South Carolina), a veteran of combat in the Waterloo Campaign against Napoleon and in the Greek War of Independence. Lieber had immigrated to the United States in 1827, fleeing political persecution in his native Prussia, and devoted himself to studying the conduct of war. A passionate supporter of the Union whose own family had been divided by the American Civil War, Lieber was uniquely qualified to codify the rules of war at the request of Abraham Lincoln's closest military advisers.[45]

Lieber argued that under the laws of war, the federal government, without recognizing the legitimacy of the Confederacy, could accord individual Confederates the privilege of belligerency, which sharply distinguished between warfare waged by the military and the fighting of noncombatants. In so doing he resolved a very thorny problem for Lincoln. But he strongly advocated that Lincoln "issue a set of rules and definitions providing for the most urgent issues occurring under the Law and usages of War." Lincoln must, "as Commander in Chief, through the Secretary of War . . . appoint a committee . . . to draw up a code . . . in which certain acts and offenses (under the Law of War) ought to be defined and, where necessary, the punishment stated."[46]

A little over a month later Lieber was appointed, together with four general officers, to a board charged with proposing "a code of regulations for the government of armies in the field, as authorized by the law and usages of war." But it was Lieber who did the lion's share of the work, and this code was quickly approved by Lincoln and issued as the official rule of conduct for the Union armies on April 24, 1863.

Lieber's opinion was that whenever feasible, civilians and their property should be shielded from the ravages of war. To do so would mean that civilians were warned well in advance to get out of harm's way and that certain institutions such as libraries and hospitals would be protected. Both Lieber and Lincoln believed that cruelty and revenge had no place in war, and Lieber insisted that soldiers pay heed to the effects that their actions would have after the guns fell silent. The code that Lincoln approved became the foundation of the modern laws of war.

Ironically, it was issued by the president at just the juncture when he was working to transform the war from one of restoration to one of reformation in the guise of the Emancipation Proclamation. Too, it was issued amid a war that became portentous of modern warfare in its mass destructive scale. "The hard hand of war" described by William T. Sherman was about to replace the limited war policies of the first two years of the Lincoln administration, and it would be theoretically governed by the words of an immigrant. Lincoln shared Lieber's tough humanitarianism, and while the president reluctantly approved the death sentences of guerrilla combatants, he repeatedly commuted such sentences to imprisonment at hard labor for the duration of the war. Lincoln found in Lieber's words the structure and sentiment, if not the solace, he had long sought in determining how to wage war against one's own countrymen.[47]

Lincoln had to deal with other war-related immigrant issues as well. Although his relationships with specific immigrant groups were cordial for the most part, the war necessitated that the president see the big picture on all issues, including immigrants. The organization and growth of the Union army and the increasing need for war materiel and supplies all served together to stimulate the Northern economy. Labor, however, remained scarce, and the last thing that Lincoln needed was a war effort crippled by strikes and labor unrest as businesses took huge profits but stubbornly refused to recognize any organization by workers designed to improve the laborer's lot.

After the firing on Fort Sumter, many of the immigrants that Lincoln had encouraged and welcomed became less than enthusiastic about his war. Germans, Irish, Jews, and other immigrants, in fact, lost even more enthusiasm once the Emancipation Proclamation was announced. The *Seebote*, a Milwaukee German language newspaper, expressed horror that European immigrants should be "used as fodder for cannons" in an abolitionist war and that under Lincoln's proclamation, the "Germans, and Irish must be annihilated, to make room for the Negro." Germans, Irishmen, Belgians, and Luxembourgers in Wisconsin rioted against the draft.[48]

So many men of foreign birth claimed draft exemption that Lincoln issued a proclamation on May 8, 1863, on that very subject. Referring to the Enrollment Act passed by Congress the previous March, Lincoln stipulated that "it was enacted by said statute that all able bodied male citizens of the United States, and persons of foreign birth who shall have declared on oath their intention to become citizens under and in pursuance of the laws thereof . . . shall be liable to perform military duty in the service of the United States when called out by the President for that purpose."[49]

In his 1863 annual message to Congress, Lincoln then refused to accept the claim of the foreign-born and those on their behalf that they were not subject to that law, and he announced that he would not accept "pleas of alienage" from any immigrant who had ever voted or who had not voted but had declared an intention of becoming a citizen and was still in this country sixty-five days after the proclamation date. "There is reason to believe," he wrote, "that many persons born in foreign countries, who have declared their intention to become citizens, or have been fully naturalized, have evaded military duty required of them by denying [that] fact, and thereby throwing upon the government the burden of proof." Lincoln went on, "There is reason to believe that foreigners frequently become citizens of the United States for the sole purpose of evading duties imposed by the laws of their native countries, to which, on becoming naturalized here, they at once repair, and though never returning to the United States, they still claim the interposition of this government as citizens."

Still, Lincoln welcomed immigrants into the United States at the same time that he was becoming increasingly annoyed with many of them for their lack of support. Immigrants could come and remain without fear of the draft so long as they took no step toward naturalization and refrained from exercising one of the rights of citizenship, the right to vote. During the first three years of the war, the immigration figures had been very low in comparison with those in the prewar years, and employers began to complain about a labor shortage. In response, Lincoln urged Congress to do something to encourage immigration, reiterating his desire to fix the immigrant and labor problems of the Union: "I again submit to your consideration the expediency of establishing a system for the encouragement of immigration. Although this source of national wealth and strength is again flowing with greater freedom than for several years before the insurrection occurred, there is still a great deficiency of laborers in every field of industry, especially in agriculture and in our mines, as well of iron and coal as of the precious metals. While the demand for labor is thus increased here, tens of thousands of persons, destitute of remunerative occupation, are thronging our foreign consulates, and offering to immigrate to the United States if essential, but very cheap, assistance can be afforded them. It is easy to see that, under the sharp discipline of civil war, the nation is beginning a new life. This noble effort demands the aid, and ought to receive the attention and support of the government."[50]

"Future historians," wrote one labor periodical, "will assign a most important place in history" to Lincoln's words. "Surely no more profitable use of the people's money could be made then in expending a moderate sum in facilitating emigration of a large number of laborers, especially skilled workers, to this country. We hope Congress will promptly do its duty but meantime let not the employers of labor remain idle, but rather by combined and systematic effort seek to influence at once an increased volume of emigration from Europe."[51]

Congress heeded Lincoln's words. The following year, appropriately on July 4, it passed the first of the federal laws regulating the admission of immigrants, titled "An act to encourage immigration" and known as the 1864 Immigration Act for short. Among other reasons, this law was created in hopes of meeting the labor shortage created by war conditions. Before leaving their native countries, immigrants to the United States could make contracts pledging their wages for a term not exceeding twelve months to repay the expense of their transportation, and those contracts were to be "valid in law" and enforceable in US courts. In another section designed to encourage European laborers to leave their homeland, it was provided that immigrants were to be exempt from military service during the war. No head tax was levied under this act, and it contained no exclusionist provisions. It was not an act to regulate immigration, but as clearly indicated in its full title, an act to encourage immigration.[52]

The president was authorized, with the advice and consent of the Senate, to appoint a commissioner of immigration for a term of four years at an annual salary of $2,500. A United States Emigrant Office was to be established in New York City under the supervision of a superintendent of immigration, whose salary was to be $2,000. His responsibilities would include making railroad and transportation contracts for tickets to be furnished to the immigrants, facilitating their travel to their destination, and enforcing the Passenger Act of 1855, which protected travelers on ships and other forms of transportation. The annual budget for the implementation of this act was to be no more than $25,000. The law was welcomed by business and agricultural concerns alike.

Regrettably, however, the law was not especially productive. In three years the Bureau of Immigration, created by the United States Emigrant Office, had four commissioners of immigration: General James Bowen, H. N. Congar, E. Peshine Smith, and R. S. Chilton. The bureau was accused of entering into a questionable relationship with such private companies as the American Emigrant Company. And indeed, when the Bureau of Immigration opened its office in New York City, it moved into the very building occupied by the American Emigrant Company. Senator Justin Morrill of Vermont attacked the bureau on the Senate floor for that very reason. "All on earth that this Bureau has done since [its inception]," Morrill fumed, "is to act in harmony and in such subordination to the emigration aid society or company . . . I submit that [this] is not a very dignified business for the Government of the United States anyway." Many complaints were filed by various European consulates that their countrymen had been lured to the United States under false pretenses and had not received either the land or the salaries that they had been promised and for which they had paid. Furthermore, Lincoln was besieged with petitions from people who wished to have the transportation fee waived. A number of Scottish handloom weavers, French workers, Austrian laborers, and many other similar cases desperately sought entrance into the United States but did not wish to contract their transportation costs. At Lincoln's request, the Bureau of Immigration replied to all such requests by explaining that it had no authority to pay for anyone's passage to America.[53]

By his 1864 annual message the president was urging Congress to amend the law, "which will enable the officers of the government to continue to prevent frauds against the immigrants while on their way and on their arrival in the ports, so as to secure them here a free choice of avocations and places of settlement." Lincoln went on to say, "A liberal disposition towards this great national policy is manifested by most of the European States, and ought to be reciprocated on our part by giving the immigrants effective national protection." In what could arguably be construed as Lincoln's most important and definitive statement on the importance of immigrants in the United States, the president asserted, "I regard our emigrants as one of the principal replenishing streams which are appointed by Providence to repair the ravages of internal war, and its wastes of national strength and health. All that is necessary is to secure the flow of that stream [of immigrants] in its present fullness, and to that end the government must, in every way, make it manifest that it neither needs nor designs to impose involuntary military service upon those who come from other lands to cast their lot in our country."[54]

Accepting Lincoln's call for action, on February 7, 1865, Representative Elihu B. Washburne introduced a bill to amend the 1864 Immigration Act. Washburne's bill gave the commissioner of immigration additional power to strengthen the passenger acts, provided more rigid penalties for violations of these laws, and gave the commissioner the power to sue and collect through the courts on all penalties. Additional US immigration offices were to be established in Boston, New Orleans, Baltimore, San Francisco, and Philadelphia, under the direction of superintendents who would have the same powers as the superintendent in New York. Washburne's bill passed the House but ran into immediate trouble in the Senate, where some members did not wish to amend the bill but instead were intent on repealing it. Consistently critical of the bill, Senator Morrill said that the government was not in the business of importing men and that it encouraged a species of slavery. Supported by other Republican senators, Morrill was able to table the measure and bury it from further discussion. This action portended the death of congressional interest in following Lincoln's suggestion that the 1864 Immigration Act be amended. The criticism of the act by Lincoln's own party in the Senate became so visceral that the Republicans began the successful movement to repeal the only act the federal government ever passed to encourage immigration.

Ironically, the Republicans who went along with Lincoln in recognizing immigration as an integral part of their economic policies would not go all the way by providing the newcomers with "the effective national protection" that he demanded. Their refusal sadly presaged the future, when the contract labor law, as it became known, which had been meant to benefit the nation in its time of need and protect foreign workers, was used, among other things, to import strikebreakers and foster an environment of hatred and prejudice toward the newly arrived immigrants. Lincoln, however, would not live to see the complete subversion of the law he once considered to be critical to the nation's economic prosperity.

Lincoln fully recognized the effect a foreign labor supply would have on wages. Yet he saw no inconsistency between his devotion to the American workingmen and his support of immigration. He was certain that the rich lands of the West, in concert with the Homestead Act, would attract scores of men and thus resolve, albeit in a minor sense, the labor shortage brought on by war. For America, with the economy ever growing, the problem had never been a glut on the labor market; it had been quite the opposite. Lincoln's attitude had a political ingredient, to be sure, but one consisting much more of future hopes than contemporary realities.

It is apparent, then, that before and during his presidency, Lincoln displayed hospitality and tolerance toward immigrants regardless of their country, culture, or creed. He invited them and welcomed them to share not only in the economic opportunity that the country offered but also in the great political experiment that he considered the United States to be. Only time would tell, he believed, whether the principles of the Declaration of Independence and the US Constitution would endure, survive, and flourish. To Lincoln, the words of those documents were intended to set up a "standard maxim for free society" to be "constantly labored for," thereby constantly "augmenting the happiness and the value of life to all people of all colors everywhere." The experiment to which he welcomed immigrants, therefore, was of vital interest to the whole "family of man."[55] His nation was a work in progress, and Lincoln sought to open its doors to those willing to uproot themselves and start over.

CERTAINTY: THE GREAT
EMANCIPATOR OR THE
GREAT EGALITARIAN?

"The only thing like passion or infatuation in the man was the passion for the Union of These States," Walt Whitman wrote of Abraham Lincoln. Lincoln's love for the Union transcended people and places. It was to him the essence of what a true democracy represented. And Whitman was indeed correct. Certainly it represented the promise of a new beginning and a brighter future for the millions of immigrants who braved the voyage to the America of Lincoln's lifetime. "He loved his country partly because it was his own country, but mostly because it was a free country; and he burned with a zeal for its advancement, prosperity, and glory, because he saw, in such, the advancement, prosperity, and glory of human liberty, human rights, and human nature. He desired the prosperity of his countrymen partly because they were his countrymen, but chiefly to show the world that freemen could be prosperous." Though these words were spoken by Abraham Lincoln in eulogizing his hero and mentor Henry Clay, they are an extremely fitting description of Lincoln himself.[1]

At the core of Lincoln's thinking were his close reading of and deep commitment to the Declaration of Independence. In fact, the Declaration of Independence was an inclusive document whose ideals welcomed and embraced newcomers of all ancestry. To accept a less inclusive interpretation would mean in effect the disfranchisement of recent immigrants who could claim equality within the white race, and Lincoln would not accept that. There must be "an open field and a fair chance," Lincoln said, for men of industry, enterprise, and intelligence. There must be an open society in which a worker, foreign-born or native-born, can rise to become an independent entrepreneur and capitalist, with his own employees, who in turn will have an opportunity to rise according to their own merits.

On many occasions Lincoln made this abundantly clear to his audience. "Chief Justice Taney, in his opinion in the Dred Scott case, admits that the language of the Declaration is broad enough to include the whole human family," Lincoln said in his speech on the Dred Scott decision, "but he and Judge [Stephen] Douglas argue that the authors of that instrument did not intend to include negroes, by the fact that they did not at once, actually place them on an equality with the whites. Now this grave argument comes to just nothing at all, by the other fact, that they did not at once, *or ever afterwards*, actually place all white people on an equality with one or another." Furthermore, Lincoln added, "I think the authors of that notable instrument intended to include *all* men, but they did not intend to declare all men equal *in all respects*. They did not mean to say all were equal in color, size, intellect, moral developments, or social capacity. They defined with tolerable distinctiveness, in what respects they did consider all men created equal—equal in 'certain inalienable rights, among which are life, liberty, and the pursuit of happiness.' This they said, and this [they] meant. They did not mean to assert the obvious untruth, that all were then actually enjoying that equality, nor yet, that they were about to confer it immediately upon them. In fact they had no power to confer such a boon." He often chided his adversaries about their misinterpretation of the document, which he considered sacrosanct. "My good friends," he said in the same speech, "read that carefully over some leisure hour, and ponder well upon it—see what a mere wreck—mangled ruin—it makes of our once glorious Declaration. 'They were speaking of British subjects born and residing in Great Britain!' Why, according to this, not only negroes but white people outside of Great Britain and America are not spoken of in that instrument. The English, Irish and Scotch, along with white Americans, were included to be sure, but the French, Germans and other white people of the world are all gone to pot along with the Judge's inferior races."[2]

In a later speech Lincoln returned to this theme: "We have Judge Douglas giving his exposition of what the Declaration of Independence means, and we have him saying that the people of America are equal to the people of England. According to his construction, you Germans are not connected with it. Now I ask you in all soberness, if all these things, if indulged in, if ratified, if confirmed and endorsed, if taught to our children, and repeated to them, do not tend to rub out the sentiment of liberty in the country, and to transform this Government into a government of some other form."[3]

Lincoln surely believed that free men could change society and the individual for the good, for he had a strong faith in material and moral progress. And what private groups could not accomplish, he thought the government should undertake. "The legitimate object of government," Lincoln said, "is to do for the people, what needs to be done, but which they can not, by individual effort, do at all, or do so well, for themselves." Lincoln was no advocate of laissez-faire and felt that if immigrants needed assistance from a strong and active federal government, then it should be provided.[4]

First and foremost, Lincoln was a politician, and that was never far from the core of his public statements about immigrants. He once derisively described politicians as "a set of men who have interests aside from the interests of the people, and who, to say the most of them, are, taken as a mass, at least one long step removed from honest men." Interestingly enough, he did not exempt himself from his cynical definition. "I say this with the greater freedom," he went on, "because, being a politician myself, none can regard it as personal."[5]

Moreover, Lincoln has been derided as a politician whose decisions were always based on the political realities of the day. Yet that is not entirely true. Lincoln was especially pragmatic and flexible on issues that concerned him the most. A man of great principle and abiding optimism for the experiment of the Founding Fathers, Lincoln believed that the Union could survive only if its beneficence could be spread to all peoples. His interpretation of Union was predicated on Lincoln's deep, abiding belief in the Declaration of Independence and what it potentially offered all, both within and without America's borders. To Lincoln, the Declaration was meant not only for those of British descent—or even those of the white race.

Both before and during his presidency, Lincoln set an example of hospitality and tolerance toward immigrants of every country, culture, or creed. He invited them to share not only in economic opportunity but also in the great political experiment that he considered the United States to be. Only time, he believed, would tell whether the principles of the Constitution and the Declaration of Independence would work permanently. The founders of the republic intended to set up a "standard maxim for free society" to be "constantly labored for" and thereby to be constantly "augmenting the happiness and value of life to all people of all colors everywhere." The experiment therefore was of vital interest to the whole "family of man" and had profound worldwide consequences. Should the American experiment of democracy fail, it would come from within, Lincoln believed. It would not be the result of foreign influences or "some transatlantic military giant, to step the Ocean, and crush us at a blow[.] Never! All the armies of Europe, Asia and Africa combined, with all the treasure of the earth (our own excepted) in their military chest; with a Buonaparte [*sic*] for a commander, could not by force, take a drink from the Ohio, or make a track on the Blue Ridge, in a trial of a thousand years. . . . If it ever reach us, it must spring up amongst us. It cannot come from abroad," Lincoln predicted. "If destruction be our lot, we must ourselves be its author and finisher. As a nation of freemen, we must live through all time, or die by suicide."[6]

The principles of the Declaration of Independence and the Constitution were, in their ultimate origin, as English "as the men who proclaimed them, as English as the language the men used to write them." But in no other country have so many different peoples come together and managed to live together so successfully. They have managed it because, on the whole, they have accepted a common core of political values—the values that Lincoln so magnificently exemplified and so eloquently expressed. Lincoln reminded his audiences that the fact that the Declaration does not specify nationality or ethnicity was not intended as a means of including only British heirs and excluding all others. Furthermore, he made it clear that unless the Declaration is read as an instrument of inclusion, the ideals of the Revolution are rendered as empty words. "I had thought the Declaration promised something better than the condition of the British subjects," Lincoln said, "but no, it only meant that we should be *equal* to them in their own oppressed and *unequal* condition. According to that, it gave no promise that having kicked off the King and the Lords of Great Britain we should not at once be saddled with a King and Lords of our own."[7]

Lincoln's opponents criticized his use of the Declaration of Independence on at least two major grounds, one charging him with an inaccurate reading of the founders' intent, the other with engaging in esoteric abstraction. States' rights advocates such as Senators John C. Calhoun and Stephen A. Douglas denied the existence of any "common moral foundation" outside of local interests and reminded Lincoln that Thomas Jefferson himself had been a slave owner who never intended his document to apply to anyone other than his fellow revolutionaries. Furthermore, they said, the guiding premise of the American Revolution, as articulated by Thomas Paine, was that tradition imposes no authority on subsequent generations, rendering Jefferson's intent meaningless. Lincoln responded to such charges with his own reminder that historical circumstance had already extended liberty and equality to Frenchmen, Irish, Germans, Jews, and other groups whom the founders probably did not intend to include. For Lincoln, the specific context of Jefferson's words mattered less than their spirit; like the Constitution, the Declaration was a living document to be reinterpreted by each generation, well in keeping with Paine's warning about the tyranny of tradition.[8]

The other charge accused Lincoln of elevating the Declaration to some abstract principle with no regard for the economic conditions of the people it purportedly liberated. Douglas raised this argument when he asked Lincoln how he could favor "natural equality" for black Americans without turning them into social and political equals. Lacking his usual eloquence, Lincoln fumbled in his attempts to reconcile the contradiction. Neither philosopher nor theologian, Lincoln did possess an exceptionally talented legal mind. And like a true conservative, he rested many of his ideas on nostalgia, and his greatest fear was that his present age was abandoning the tradition of natural rights enshrined by the founding generation. Lincoln's usage of the term "natural equality" was consistent with that of earlier Western thinkers who saw natural rights as an extension of natural law, and when he used the term, he was resurrecting more the meaning established by John Locke than that of anyone else. For Locke, the rights to be free from harm, robbery, enslavement, or killing and to enjoy the fruits of one's own labor were absolute. To Lincoln, these things were precisely what immigrants would obtain when they sought citizenship and a brighter future in the United States.

Lincoln's interpretation of the Declaration was essentially Lockean, and his reading of it may in fact have been closer to Locke's intent than that of Jefferson's. In Lincoln's time this argument amounted to a debate as to whether nonwhites met the criteria for natural rights laid out by the Enlightenment thinkers. As the Declaration's chief defender, Lincoln's own answer to that question was much more easily answered in regard to immigrants than to slaves.[9]

More important to Lincoln than Locke, though, was the Whig Party and the powerful influence it exerted over Lincoln and the Republican Party. During the US-Mexican War the majority of Whigs had readily accepted the idea that "Americans" were superior within the white race, yet they saw the use of that superiority as an immoral force against weaker, inferior nonwhite people such as the Mexicans. The thoughts of Lincoln's ideological and political role model, Henry Clay, directed Lincoln. The two Westerners shared many of the same racist ideas about white people and nonwhite people, about slavery and freedom. It was within this mindset that Lincoln developed his blind spot and prejudice toward Hispanics.

However, though Lincoln and Clay might have shared a belief in black and Hispanic inferiority, in their eyes the belief was irrelevant when weighed against the basic humanity of these people. Put simply, white supremacy did not justify the unlawful domination of nonwhite people. Lincoln especially equated the denial of economic rights for immigrants, laborers, and slaves with Europe's aristocratic system of hereditary privilege. "This argument strikes me as not a little remarkable in another particular—in its strong resemblance to the old argument for the 'Divine rights of King,'" Lincoln said. "By the latter, the King is to do just as he pleases with his white subjects, being responsible to God alone. By the former the white man is to do just as he pleases with his black slaves, being responsible to God Alone. The two things are precisely alike; and it is but natural that they should find similar arguments to sustain them." Such attacks were consistent with Lincoln's broad reading of the Declaration, casting his opposition to both slavery and prejudice toward immigrants within a much wider American political tradition of the struggle against false privilege.[10]

To Lincoln, the Declaration provided America with unifying principles that he hoped would lead it to welcome newcomers into its midst. His words in the Gettysburg Address, "Our fathers brought forth on this continent, a new nation, conceived in liberty, and dedicated to the proposition that all men are created equal," demonstrated clearly that Lincoln understood the Lockean definition of equality better than did the Declaration's author, Thomas Jefferson. For Jefferson equality and natural rights extended only as far as white male citizens and did not give a nod at all toward future immigrants.

In contrast to Jefferson, who praised agricultural labor but favored a "natural aristocracy," Lincoln put a premium on hard work, diligence, and perseverance and felt the system should reward those who sought to avail themselves of any chance to rise out of poverty. And immigrants fit this description precisely. "I want every man to have a chance . . . ," Lincoln said, "in which he can better his condition—when he may look forward and hope to be a hired laborer this year and next, work for himself afterward, and finally to hire men to work for him! That is the true system."[11]

Lincoln's declaration that he wanted "every man to have a chance" was his homage to the American Dream. Speaking in Cincinnati to a group of German immigrants, Lincoln extolled the virtues of that dream in no uncertain terms. "Working men are the basis of all governments," he asserted. "That remark is due to them more than to any other class. . . . [And] on behalf of workingmen, but especially of Germans, I may say a word as to classes. I hold [that] the value of life is to improve one's condition. Whatever is calculated to advance the condition of the honest, struggling laboring man, so far as my judgment will enable me to judge of a correct thing, I am for that thing."[12] Lincoln's sentiment then, transcended race, gender, and ethnicity, for it was an economic theory based on equal opportunity for all.

Lincoln knew that European immigrants desired to achieve the American Dream even while clinging to their Old World cultures and traditions, and he extended to them without hesitation both the Homestead Law, which made available to them plots of lands in the territories, and the Declaration, which secured for them their natural, inalienable rights. Lincoln understood full well the destructive power and the danger of arguing over who constituted a "real" American. "Let us discard all this quibbling about this man and the other man," Lincoln said, "this race and that race and the other race as being inferior, and therefore they must be placed in an inferior position—discarding our standard that we have left us. Let us discard all these things, and unite as one people throughout this land, until we shall once more stand up declaring that all men are created equal."[13]

To accomplish this, Lincoln fervently believed that Americans should "duly appreciate the value of [their] free institutions." He argued that it was precisely because America happened to enjoy political freedom that the country should be open to different peoples everywhere. The Declaration, he emphasized, offered "liberty, not alone to the people of this country, but hope to the world for all future time. It was that which gave promise that in due time the weights should be lifted from the shoulders of all men, and that, *all* should have an equal chance. This is the sentiment embodied in that Declaration of Independence. . . . If [this country] can't be saved upon that principle, it will be truly awful. But if this country cannot be saved without giving up that principle—I was about to say I would rather be assassinated on this spot than to surrender it." The development of republican liberty in Lincoln's America represented the "last best hope of earth" to the whole "family of man," for the idea of self-government, if it could withstand the test of the Civil War, had the potential to "liberate the world."[14]

Compared with many of his contemporaries, Lincoln possessed a distinctly different opinion of what it meant to be an American.

To him, it was a matter of commitment to certain principles, not a matter of racial or cultural inheritance. To become an American—to become a citizen of the United States—an immigrant "should be put to some reasonable test of his [or her] fidelity to our country and its institutions," and he or she "should first dwell among us a reasonable time to become generally acquainted with the nature of those institutions." So Lincoln believed. And the "naturalization laws should be so framed as to render admission to citizenship under them as convenient, cheap and expeditious as possible." It was the duty of the elected official, Lincoln maintained, to "oppose as best we may, all attempts to either destroy the naturalization laws or to so alter them" as to make citizenship for immigrants more difficult. Thus in Lincoln's view it should be fairly easy to become an American, regardless of the immigrant's native country or culture.[15]

In his life, then, Lincoln rose to condemn discriminatory immigration or naturalization policies when they were advocated. Though he walked a very thin political tightrope, he had opposed the Know Nothings when they advocated their rabid anti-immigrant policies. He wrote to his political ally Owen Lovejoy that regrettably the Know Nothings had "not yet tumbled to pieces." Uncomfortably for Lincoln, they were "mostly my old political and personal friends," he wrote; "and I had hoped that their organization would die out without the painful necessity of taking an open stand against them." Yet in the end his principles prevailed over his politics, and he did have to oppose the Know Nothings in their anti-Irish and anti-German crusade, writing to Lovejoy, "I do not perceive how anyone professing to be sensitive to the wrongs of the negroes, can join in a league to degrade a class of white men."[16]

This attitude toward the immigrant transcended Lincoln's mere political life. Years after his assassination an attorney recalled trying to engage Lincoln as co-counsel on a case to deprive some immigrants of their vote. "I heard Lincoln say about 1858—say in October," recalled Charles S. Zane, "that the Know-nothings—their ideas & platform wanted to circumscribe the Election franchise—universal Suffrage. That [Lincoln] was opposed to it—That he wanted to lift men up & give 'Em a chance. . . . I am opposed to limitation [he said]—the lessening of the right of suffrage—am in favor of its Extension—enlargement—want to lift men up and broaden them—don't intend by no act of mine to Crush or Contract."[17] This decision did not come cheaply, and Lincoln was very aware that his position on immigration could cost him votes, which it did when the Know Nothings refused to support him in 1854 because of his stand against them.

Undaunted, Lincoln genuinely believed that the United States was unique in the history of the world. Here was a "government of a system of political institutions conducing more essentially to the ends of civil and religious liberty than any of which the history of former times tells us," Lincoln maintained. In his very first political statement, as a young man of twenty-three, Lincoln proposed that everyone "receive at least, a moderate education, and thereby be enabled to read the histories of his own and other countries, by which he may duly appreciate the value of our free institutions." Lincoln envisioned that the United States would be a beacon of hope for people from all around the world. Once here, through hard work and virtue, the newcomers could thrive in a land of opportunity and unbridled economic potential. Long before the Statue of Liberty was erected, Lincoln was articulating what it would represent to the immigrants and their dreams.[18]

In a time when hatred of one group or another dominated, Lincoln sought to temper prejudice and mitigate conflict. Like a great many other Americans, Lincoln was appalled by the 1863 New York City draft riots, in which Irish immigrants attacked African Americans. When, several months later, he was elected an honorary member of the New York Workingmen's Association, he responded with some advice for his fellow members: "Let [laborers] beware of prejudice, working division and hostility among themselves. The most notable feature of a disturbance on your city last summer was the hanging of some working people by other working people. It should never be so. The strongest bonds of human sympathy, outside of the family relation, should be one uniting all working people, of all nations, and tongues, and kindreds."[19]

Historians have given Lincoln credit for his reading of the founding documents and his ability to modernize them for his times. As one historian put it, "This view enables moral and political thought to aspire to that which is universal rather than particular; that which is necessary instead of contingent; eternal truths and timeless ideals rather than transitory facts and shifting historical contexts."[20] While pertinent, this description of Lincoln's intellectual approach to the issue of the Declaration and its legacy was more sophisticated than he would have wanted. "The world," Lincoln wrote in his inimitable way, "has never had a good definition of the word liberty, and the American people, just now, are such in the want of one. We all declare for liberty; but in using the same *word* we do not all mean the same *thing*. With some the word liberty may mean for each man to do as he pleases with himself, and the product of his labor; while with others the same word may mean for some men to do as they please with other men, and the product of other men's labor. Here are two, not only different, but incompatible things, called by the same name—liberty. And it follows that each of the things is, by the respective parties, called by two different and incompatible names—liberty and tyranny."

Yet in an analogy that is vintage Lincoln, the president went on to vividly describe the perils of being an immigrant, or minority, in his America: "The shepherd drives the wolf from the sheep's throat, for which the sheep thanks the shepherd as a *liberator*, while the wolf denounces him for the same act as a destroyer of liberty. . . . Plainly the sheep and the wolf are not agreed upon the definition of the word liberty; and precisely the same difference prevails to-day among us human creatures, even in the North, and all professing to love liberty. Hence we behold the processes by which thousands are daily passing from under the yoke of bondage, hailed by some as the advance of liberty, and bewailed by others as the destruction of all liberty." For the immigrant or the slave, the Declaration of Independence represented something distinctly different than it had to the founders, who wrote it, and Lincoln's interpretation, while not especially popular even among some in his own party, demonstrated that he understood the future of America quite clearly.[21]

Progressive though he was, Lincoln was not completely an egalitarian. For him, the Declaration was no manifesto for social leveling. Rather, in some ways it was just the opposite: it established the principle, not the promise, of equality. The founders "meant simply to declare the right [to equality], so the enforcement of it might follow as fast as circumstances should permit. They meant to set up a standard maxim for free society, which should be familiar to all, and revered by all; constantly looked to, constantly labored for, and even though never perfectly attained, constantly approximated, and thereby constantly spreading and deepening its influence, and augmenting the happiness and value of life to all people of all colors everywhere." Additionally, Lincoln saw that the phrase "all men are created equal" was meant not so much for the revolutionary generation as it was for the succeeding generations. "Its authors meant it to be," Lincoln said, "thank God it is now proving itself, a stumbling block to those who in after times might seek to turn a free people back into the hateful paths of despotism. They knew the proneness of prosperity to breed tyrants, and they meant when such should re-appear in this fair land and commerce their vocation they should find left for them at least one hard nut to crack."[22]

It is apparent that Lincoln, then, was both a mirror of his present and a beacon of the future, holding in many ways the dominant prejudiced views of his day but demonstrating clearly a capacity for intellectual growth. An angry Pennsylvania man sent him a telegram in 1864 urging his attention "to understand what is justice & what is truth to all men. . . . Equal Rights & Justice to all white men in the United States forever. White men is in class number one & black men is in class number two & must be governed by white men forever." In response, Lincoln drafted a sharp reply through John Nicolay, one of his secretaries: "I will thank you to inform me for his [the president's] use, whether you are a white man or black one, because in either case, you can not be regarded as an entirely partial judge. It may be that you belong to a third or fourth class of *yellow* or *red* men, in which case the impartiality of your judgment would be more apparent."[23]

It is not a stretch to say that Lincoln completed much of the work that the Founding Fathers had left undone. He offered an expansive reading of the Declaration of Independence that embraced immigrants who were not English, and he embraced a commitment to natural rights and humanity that extended to people of various colors, religions, creeds, and cultures. It has been said of Lincoln that his gift lay in his ability to determine the moods and prejudices of his constituencies and act in accordance with what he thought their political will would support. This might be too simplistic, if not downright unfair. Lincoln was a man of his time. He had the faults of a person raised in a society in which privilege accrued to the native-born white Anglo-Saxon male. But his life was one of transformation as he came to recognize the folly of racism and nativism in the face of the promise of equality. Lincoln found the American identity not in blood, but in belief.

For Lincoln, a just society did not require the elimination of personal prejudice, but rather it required the rendering of such prejudices as irrelevant to the public sphere. Such ideals still hold valuable lessons for a nation that has grown ever more complicated and diverse since Lincoln's death, with regard to not only color but also language, national origin, religious belief, and sexual preference. To conceive of a prejudice-free society in such an environment—where even one American would witness the multiplicity of belief systems and subcultures and judge them as equal to his or her own—would seem a naïve, utopian fantasy to a pragmatist like Lincoln.

As a politician, and as an individual, Lincoln chose when, where, and to what extent he would provide his support to those who needed it. Consequently, taken as a whole, some of his statements on immigration and ethnicity seem at odds with others. But one thing cannot be ignored: Abraham Lincoln treated most people and groups with equal consideration. Certainly he was not immune to many of the common thoughts of his time regarding people of different colors and creeds. What set Lincoln apart from most of his countrymen, however, was his ability to look past what his society told him a person or group must be like and trust his own assessments instead. This is precisely what most Americans of Lincoln's generation could not do then, and many cannot do now. And perhaps therein lies the former rail-splitter's greatest contribution.

ACKNOWLEDGMENTS

I have been fascinated with Abraham Lincoln since the fourth grade, when I portrayed Stephen A. Douglas in a silent vignette dramatizing the famous Lincoln-Douglas debates. Regrettably, I was not tall enough to be Abe. And I want to thank Richard W. Etulain, Sara Vaughn Gabbard, and Sylvia Frank Rodrigue for inviting me to contribute a volume to the Concise Lincoln Library and thereby fulfilling a career-long wish to write a book on Lincoln. Sylvia, in particular, supported this project from its genesis and always offered words of support and encouragement. She is an absolute delight to work with. I am indebted to all three editors for their valuable comments on the manuscript, and I thank them, as well as the anonymous reader, for making suggestions on improving my work. I am amazed at the degree to which my copy editor, Joyce Bond, improved my manuscript. She and Wayne Larsen, project editor at the press, prevented a number of my embarrassing and lazy missteps.

This book could not have been written or researched without the generosity of the Ellison Capers Palmer Jr. Professorship. At a time when Winthrop University faculty and staff went six out of seven years without any salary increase, the financial support of the Palmer Professorship quite literally meant the difference between undertaking this study and not. What Winthrop's Dacus Library lacks in size, it makes up for with wonderful people. Jean Wells in Interlibrary Loan and Nancy White in Circulation processed all of my requests for volumes, newspapers, theses, and dissertations successfully and expeditiously, and I am very thankful for all of their hard work. James Cornelius, Mary Michals, and Jennifer Ericson of the Abraham Lincoln Presidential Library and Museum provided assistance and photographs at key intervals of my work, and I am very much appreciative. Jonathan Eaker at the Library of Congress did yeoman duty for me and found a picture of Theodore Canisius when no one else could. Tanya Elder and Heather Halliday of the American Jewish Historical Society and Boni-Dari Michaels of the Yeshiva University Museum promptly and efficiently helped me obtain a photograph of Dr. Isachar Zacharie, for which I am grateful.

I have waited my entire academic career for a chairman like Gregory Crider. No one at Winthrop was more enthusiastic or supportive of my work than Greg, who not only read the entire manuscript and offered excellent suggestions but also listened to me talk endlessly about Lincoln during our regular, and sustaining, lunches. In a very short time Greg became one of my closest and most trusted friends. Both Greg and I waited for an administrative assistant like Elizabeth Oswald, my former student, to come along. For four years, she skillfully handled the egos and demands of two departments. She cheerfully made everyone's life easier, but she was indispensable to me, and every day I was grateful for her presence in the History Department. My racquetball partner for more than a quarter of a century, Bob Gorman, a baseball scholar par excellence, read the manuscript and offered a number of good ideas. Bob and I together have matured from young turks to elder statesmen (I can't write senior citizens!) over the years in the gym, and I could always count on him to provide friendship and competitive racquetball. No one is more reliable than Bob.

Bruce Levine, Frank Williams, Jason Emerson, Tom Turner, and Kevin Kenny all took time out of their very busy and full schedules to read my manuscript, and my book is so much the better for it. Their suggestions and corrections saved me from a number of infelicities, and any flaws remaining are due to my stubbornness and not their incisive comments. Bruce and Kevin generously shared with me prepublication versions of their essays, which helped me quite a bit. As editor of the *Lincoln Herald*, Tom was the first to see the value in my work, and it is only fitting that my first published words on Lincoln and the immigrant appeared in that premier Lincoln studies journal. Truly, Bruce, Frank, Jason, Tom, and Kevin all personify what it means to be gentlemen and scholars.

For thirty years my wife, Susan, has read every word that I've written and improved them each time. Besides her own myriad activities, first as head of public services in Winthrop's Dacus Library and now as director of library assessment, Susan manages endless chores at home for me and our son, Alex, which makes it possible for me to write and think about Abraham Lincoln. No human being I have ever met is more patient and selfless than Susan. I wish I could be more like her. When Alex was a little boy, he constantly reminded me of more important things to do in life by requesting that I play with him. He has now grown into a remarkable young man of such honesty, integrity, courage, and principle that I wish I could be more like him too. And thankfully he still reminds me of more important things to do outside my world of the nineteenth century.

My students in the several semesters of the senior history majors' seminar that I taught on Abraham Lincoln likely heard more about my work than they cared to, and in return they wanted to be mentioned in my book. No student in my teaching career was more generous than my friend and indefatigable old warrior Dick Davis. Thanks to his generosity, my library and my wardrobe have been enhanced significantly. It is to him and to the thousands of Winthrop students I have taught over thirty years that I dedicate this book.

NOTES

Introduction

1. James G. Randall, "Has the Lincoln Theme Been Exhausted?," *American Historical Review* 41 (January 1936): 270–94; Clyde C. Walton, "An Agonizing Reappraisal: 'Has the Lincoln Theme Been Exhausted?,'" in *Lincoln Images: Augustana College Centennial Essays*, ed. O. Fritiof Ander (Rock Island, IL: Augustana College Library, 1960), 99–105.

2. *Wall Street Journal*, October 12, 2012.

3. A very interesting essay on immigration by Kevin Kenny appears in *A Companion to Abraham Lincoln*, ed. Michael S. Green (Malden, MA: Blackwell Publishing, forthcoming). Richard Striner, *Lincoln and Race* (Carbondale: Southern Illinois University Press, 2012) includes much material that greatly informed my study.

4. Henry C. Whitney, *Lincoln, The Citizen: The Life of Abraham Lincoln* (New York: Baker and Taylor Co., 1908), 1:22; Michael J. O'Brien, *Irish Settlers in America* (Baltimore: Genealogical Publishing Co., 1979), 2:95; Ida M. Tarbell, *The Early Life of Abraham Lincoln* (1896; repr., South Brunswick, NJ: A.S. Barnes and Company, 1974), 46–47.

5. Christine Kinealy, *Private Charity to Ireland during the Great Hunger: The Kindness of Strangers* (London: Bloomsbury, 2012); "Memories and Recollections of Susan Man McCulloch, 1818–1898," manuscript in the Abraham Lincoln Presidential Library and Museum, Springfield, IL, 30; Abraham Lincoln, "Speech in the United States House of Representatives on Internal Improvements," June 20, 1848, in *The Collected Works of Abraham Lincoln*, ed. Roy P. Basler, (New Brunswick, NJ: Rutgers University Press, 1953), 1:480–90. See also Noel Ignatiev, *How the Irish Became White* (New York: Routledge Publishing, 1995).

6. Francis Fisher Browne, *The Every-Day Life of Abraham Lincoln*, rev. ed. (Chicago: Browne and Howell Company, 1913), 270–72.

7. Olivier Frayssé, *Lincoln, Land, and Labor, 1809–1860*, trans. Sylvia Neely (Urbana: University of Illinois Press, 1994).

8. The most important study of this remains G. S. Boritt, *Lincoln and the Economics of the American Dream* (Memphis: Memphis State University Press, 1978), one of the most significant works on Lincoln ever published.

9. *Illinois State Register*, June 21, 1844; Lincoln, "Speech to Germans at Cincinnati, Ohio," February 12, 1861, "Response to a Serenade," November 10, 1864, and "Annual Message to Congress," December 6, 1864, *Collected Works*, 4:201–3, 8:100–102, 136–53.

10. Lincoln, "Annual Message to Congress," December 8, 1863, *Collected Works*, 7:36–53.

11. William H. Herndon and Jesse W. Weik, *Herndon's Lincoln*, eds. Douglas L. Wilson and Rodney O. Davis (Urbana: Knox College Lincoln Studies Center and the University of Illinois Press, 2006), 120; Tyler Dennett, ed., *Lincoln and the Civil War in the Diaries and Letters of John Hay* (New York: Dodd, Mead, 1939), 143.

12. Lincoln, "Address to the New Jersey Senate at Trenton, New Jersey," February 21, 1861, and "Speech in Independence Hall, Philadelphia, Pennsylvania," February 22, 1861, *Collected Works*, 4:235–36, 240–41.

13. David Homer Bates, *Lincoln in the Telegraph Office* (New York: Century Co., 1907), 41.

1. Uncertainty: A Clash of Images

1. Nels Hokanson, *Swedish Immigrants in Lincoln's Time* (New York: Harper & Brothers Publishers, 1942), 158.

2. Douglas L. Wilson and Rodney O. Davis, eds., *Herndon's Informants: Letters, Interviews, and Statements about Abraham Lincoln* (Urbana: University of Illinois Press, 1998), 457.

3. G. S. Boritt, *Lincoln and the Economics of the American Dream* (Memphis: Memphis State University Press, 1978), 8, 27, 98; Richard Campanella, *Lincoln in New Orleans: The 1828–1831 Flatboat Voyages and Their Place in History* (Lafayette: University of Louisiana at Lafayette Press, 2010).

4. Louis A. Warren, ed., "President Lincoln's Interest in Catholic Institutions," *Lincoln Lore: Bulletin of the Lincoln National Life Foundation* 790 (May 29, 1944); Louis A. Warren, ed., "Lincoln in New Orleans," ibid. 333 (August 26, 1935).

5. William Darby, *Geographical Description of the State of Louisiana* (New York: James Olmstead, 1817), 75.

6. *New-Orleans Directory and Register* (New Orleans: J. A. Paxton, 1822), 45–46.

7. W. D. Howells, *Life of Abraham Lincoln* (Columbus: Follett, Foster and Co., 1860), 25.

8. *History of Sangamon Country, Illinois, Together with Sketches of Its Cities, Villages, and Townships* (Chicago: Inter-state Publishing Company, 1881), 736–37.

9. William Florville to Abraham Lincoln, December 27, 1863, Abraham Lincoln Papers, Library of Congress, Washington, DC; misspellings in original.

10. J. G. Holland, *The Life of Lincoln* (Springfield, MA: Gurdon Bill, 1866), 127–28.

11. Benjamin F. Jonas to Abraham Lincoln, June 4, 1857, Abraham Lincoln Papers.

12. Abraham Lincoln to Abraham Jonas, February 4, 1860, *Collected Works*, 3:516.

13. Abraham Lincoln to Abraham Jonas, August 2, 1858, ibid., 2:533–34.

14. Abraham Lincoln to Abraham Jonas, July 21, 1860, ibid., 4:85–86.

15. Abraham Jonas to Abraham Lincoln, December 30, 1860, Abraham Lincoln Papers.

16. Orville Browning to Abraham Lincoln, December 9, 1860, Robert Todd Lincoln Papers, Manuscript Division, Library of Congress, Washington, DC.

17. Lincoln, "Order for Parole of Charles H. Jonas," June 2, 1864, *Collected Works*, 7:373; Bertram W. Korn, *American Jewry and the Civil War* (Philadelphia: Jewish Publication Society, 1951), 194.

18. "As in Years Gone By," *Chicago Daily*, February 13, 1895, 5.

19. Abraham Lincoln to Martin S. Morris, March 26, 1843, *Collected Works*, 1:319–20.

20. Lincoln, "Speech at New Haven," March 6, 1860, ibid., 4:24–25.

21. *Rock Island (IL) Weekly Republican*, August 19, 1854; *Knoxville (IL) Republican*, May 13, 1856.

22. Hokanson, *Swedish Immigrants*, 54; William H. Herndon and Jesse W. Weik, *Herndon's Lincoln*, ed. Douglas L. Wilson and Rodney O. Davis (Urbana: University of Illinois Press, 2006), 15.

23. Lincoln, "Speech at Indianapolis, Indiana," September 19, 1859, *Collected Works*, 3:463–70.

24. Hokanson, *Swedish Immigrants*, 57.

25. *Chicago Press and Tribune*, October 25, November 2, 1858.

26. *Galesburg (IL) Democrat*, March 9, 1860.

27. Madeleine Vinton Dahlgren, *Memoir of John A. Dahlgren* (Boston: James R. Osgood and Company, 1882), 434–91.

28. *Sangamo Journal*, June 20, 1844; *Illinois State Register*, June 21, 1844; Lincoln, "Speech and Resolutions Concerning Philadelphia Riots," June 12, 1844, *Collected Works*, 1:337–38.

29. Rodney O. Davis and Douglas L. Wilson, eds., *The Lincoln-Douglas Debates* (Urbana: University of Illinois Press, 2008), 131.

30. Lincoln, "Speech in the United States House of Representatives: The War with Mexico," January 12, 1848, *Collected Works*, 1:431–42; Mark E. Neely Jr., "Lincoln and the Mexican War: An Argument by Analogy," *Civil War History* 26 (March 1978): 5–24; Mark E. Neely Jr., "War and Partisanship: What Lincoln Learned from James K. Polk," *Journal of the Illinois State Historical Society* 74 (Fall 1981): 199–216; David Herbert Donald, *Lincoln* (New York: Simon and Schuster, 1995), 122–26; Amy

S. Greenberg, *A Wicked War: Polk, Clay, Lincoln, and the 1846 U.S. Invasion of Mexico* (New York: Alfred A. Knopf, 2012), 248–49, 262–63.

31. Lincoln, "Fifth Debate with Stephen A. Douglas, at Galesburg, Illinois," October 7, 1858, *Collected Works*, 3: 235. See also Robert E. May, *Slavery, Race, and Conquest in the Tropics: Lincoln, Douglas, and the Future of Latin America* (New York: Cambridge University Press, 2013).

32. Lincoln, "Speech to the Springfield Scott Club," August 14, 26, 1852, and "Second Lecture on Discoveries and Inventions," February 11, 1859, *Collected Works*, 2:135–57, 3:356–63; May, *Slavery, Race and Conquest*, 205–77.

33. Lincoln, "Second Lecture on Discoveries and Inventions," February 11, 1859, *Collected Works*, 3:356–63.

34. John Patrick Diggins, *On Hallowed Ground: Abraham Lincoln and the Foundations of American History* (New Haven, CT: Yale University Press, 2000), 152–58.

35. David R. Roediger, *The Wages of Whiteness: Race and the Making of the American Working Class* (London: Verso Press, 1991), 142–43; James N. Leiker, "The Difficulties of Understanding Abe: Lincoln's Reconciliation of Racial Inequality and Natural Rights," in *Lincoln Emancipated: The President and the Politics of Race*, ed. Brian R. Dirck (DeKalb: Northern Illinois University Press, 2007), 73–99.

36. Lincoln, "Speech at Carlinville, Illinois," August 31, 1858, *Collected Works*, 3:77–81.

37. Lincoln, "Third Debate with Stephen A. Douglas at Jonesboro, Illinois," September 15, 1858, and "Fifth Debate with Stephen A. Douglas," October 7, 1858, ibid., 3:102–44, 207–44.

38. Lincoln, "Address before the Wisconsin State Agricultural Society, Milwaukee, Wisconsin," September 30, 1859, ibid., 3:471–82.

2. Awakening: Coming of Age in Springfield

1. Abraham Lincoln to Mary S. Owens, May 7, 1837, *Collected Works*, 1:78–79; Paul M. Angle, *"Here I Have Lived": A History of Lincoln's Springfield, 1821–1865* (Springfield, IL: Abraham Lincoln Association, 1935), 35, 59; Kenneth J. Winkle, *The Young Eagle: The Rise of Abraham Lincoln* (Dallas: Taylor Publishing Co., 2001), which includes very useful social data about Lincoln's Springfield.

2. Raymond Lohne, "Team of Friends: A New Lincoln Theory and Legacy," *Journal of the Illinois State Historical Society* 101 (Fall–Winter 2008), 3.

3. Ferdinand Ernst, "Travels in Illinois in 1819," *Transactions of the Illinois Historical Society* 8 (1903), 155–59; Paul E. Stroble Jr., "Ferdinand Ernst and the German Colony at Vandalia," *Illinois Historical Journal* (Summer 1987), 108.

4. Paul Simon, *Lincoln's Preparation for Greatness: The Illinois Legislative Years* (Chicago: University of Illinois Press, 1971); William E. Baringer, *Lincoln's Vandalia* (New Brunswick, NJ: Rutgers University Press, 1949).

5. *Seventh Census of the United States, 1850* (Washington, DC: Robert Armstrong, Public Printing, 1853), 705.

6. William E. Barton, *The Influence of Chicago upon Abraham Lincoln* (Chicago: University of Chicago Press, 1923), 8–30; Bruce Levine, *The Spirit of 1848: German Immigrants, Labor Conflict, and the Coming of the Civil War* (Urbana: University of Illinois Press, 1992); Mischa Honeck, *We Are the Revolutionists: German-Speaking Immigrants and the American Abolitionists after 1848* (Athens: University of Georgia Press, 2011, 159–69.

7. Angle, *"Here I Have Lived."*

8. John R. Edison, "German Club Life as a Local Cultural System," *Comparative Studies in Society and History* 32 (March 1955), 357–82.

9. Wayne C. Temple, "A.W. French: Lincoln Family Dentist," *Lincoln Herald* 63 (Fall 1961): 151–54.

10. Abraham Lincoln to Friedrich K. F. Hecker, September 14, 1856, *Collected Works*, 4:61–62.

11. George S. Hecker and James E. Gleichert, "Lincoln Writes to Friedrich Hecker: A New Letter," *Lincoln Herald* 69 (Winter 1967): 159–61.

12. Lincoln, "Speech at Belleville, Illinois, October, 18, 1856" and Abraham Lincoln to Anton C. Hesing, Henry Wendt, Alexander Fisher, Committee, June 30, 1858, *Collected Works*, 2:379–80, 475.

13. Franklin William Scott, *Newspapers and Periodicals of Illinois, 1814–1879* (Springfield: Illinois State Historical Society Library, 1910), 8.

14. Carl Sandburg, *Abraham Lincoln: The Prairie Years* (New York: Harcourt, Brace, 1926), 2:37, 259–60.

15. Wayne C. Temple, "The Linguistic Lincolns: A New Lincoln Letter," *Lincoln Herald* 94 (Fall 1994): 108–14; Frank Baron, *Abraham Lincoln and the German Immigrants: Tuners and Forty-Eighters* (Topeka: Society for German-American Studies, 2012), 77–109.

16. Abraham Lincoln to Theodore Canisius, May 17, 1859, and Lincoln, "Contract with Theodore Canisius," May [30?], 1859, *Collected Works*, 3:380–81, 383–84.

17. Isaac Markens, "Lincoln and the Jews," *Publications of the American Jewish Historical Society* 17 (1909): 137–38.

18. Dean R. Esslinger, *Immigrants and the City: Ethnicity and Mobility in a Nineteenth Century Midwestern Community* (London: Kennikat Press, 1975), 125.

19. Mark Wyman, *Immigrants in the Valley: Irish, Germans, and Americans in the Upper Mississippi Country, 1830–1860* (Chicago: Nelson-Hall, 1984), 1–17.

20. Michael Burlingame, *Abraham Lincoln: A Life*, 2 vols. (Baltimore: The Johns Hopkins University Press, 2008), 1: 546.

21. Abraham Lincoln to Norman B. Judd, October 20, 1858, *Collected Works*, 3:329–30.

22. Lincoln, "Speech at Meredosia, Illinois," October 18, 1858, ibid., 3:328–29; Dennis M. Smith, *Abraham Lincoln and the New Immigrant Irish in 1860s America* (Fort Lauderdale, FL: Nova Southeastern University, 2003); Christian G. Samito, *Becoming American under Fire: Irish Americans, African Americans, and the Politics of Citizenship during the Civil War Era* (Ithaca, NY: Cornell University Press, 2009).

23. *New York Tribune*, February 15, 1867.

24. Christopher Elliot Wallace, "The Opportunity to Grow: Springfield, Illinois during the 1850s" (PhD diss., Purdue University, 1983), 78–131.

25. *Springfield Illinois Journal*, May 11, June 22, 1848.

26. David J. Langum, *Antonio de Mattos and the Protestant Portuguese Community in Antebellum Illinois* (Jacksonville, IL: Morgan County Historical Society, 2006), 55.

27. Sandburg, *Abraham Lincoln*, 2:271.

28. Alonzo Rothschild, *"Honest Abe": A Study in Integrity Based on the Early Life of Abraham Lincoln* (Boston: Houghton Mifflin, 1917), 185–87.

29. Harry E. Pratt, *The Personal Finances of Abraham Lincoln* (Springfield, IL: Abraham Lincoln Association, 1943), 77.

30. Jordan D. Fiore, "Mr. Lincoln's Portuguese Neighbors," *Lincoln Herald* 73 (September 1971): 150–55.

31. Lloyd Ostendorf and Walter Oleksy, eds., *Lincoln's Unknown Private Life: An Oral History by His Black Housekeeper, Mariah Vance, 1850–1860*, 2 vols. (Mamaroneck, NY: Hastings House Publishing, 1995). This controversial book, edited by two respected scholars, has come under fire for the legitimacy of many of Vance's accounts. See also Sanford J. Mock, "Abraham Lincoln and the Second Portuguese Church," *Financial History* 80 (Winter 2004): 25–26, for further confirmation.

32. Robert S. Frisch, "Salzenstein's Store: Abraham Lincoln Shopped Here," *Chicago Jewish History* 26 (Winter 2002): 6–7; Emily Jane Levy, "My Family," manuscript in the Jacob Rader Marcus Center of the American Jewish Archives, Cincinnati, quoted in Gary Phillip Zola, "'He Was like One of Us': The Judaization of Abraham Lincoln," *Jewish Historical Society of South Carolina* 16 (Spring 2011): 8–10; Gary Phillip Zola, ed., *"We Called Him Rabbi Abraham": Lincoln and American Jewry. A Documentary History* (Carbondale: Southern Illinois University Press, 2014), 1–43.

3. Enlightenment: Keeping Afloat in the Era of Know Nothings

1. *Campaign Bee*, October 1855, quoted in Ernest McKay, *Henry Wilson: Practical Radical: A Portrait of a Politician* (Port Washington, NY: Kennikat Press, 1971), 92–93.

2. Bruce M. Cole, "The Chicago Press and the Know Nothings" (master's thesis, University of Chicago, 1948), 28–38. By far the best book on this subject is Tyler Anbinder, *Nativism and Slavery: The Northern Know Nothings and the Politics of the 1850s* (New York: Oxford University Press, 1992). Anyone interested in this topic must begin with this seminal book.

3. William E. Gienapp, *The Origins of the Republican Party, 1852–1856* (New York: Oxford University Press, 1987); Matthew Pinsker, "Not Always Such a Whig: Abraham Lincoln's Partisan Realignment in the 1850s," *Journal of the Abraham Lincoln Association* 29 (summer 2008): 417–40; Kenneth J. Winkle, "The Second Party System in Lincoln's Springfield," *Civil War History* 44 (December 1998): 267–84.

4. Noah Levering, "Recollections of Abraham Lincoln," *Iowa Historical Record* 12 (July 1896): 495–97.

5. Otto R. Kyle, *Abraham Lincoln in Decatur* (New York: Vantage Press, 1957), 72.

6. Gustave Koerner, *The Memoirs of Gustave Koerner, 1809–1896: Life Sketches Written at the Suggestion of His Children*, ed. Thomas J. McCormick (Cedar Rapids, IA: Torch Press, 1909), 1:444. A very interesting new book that I was able to review in manuscript form is Donald Allendorf, *"Your Friend, As Ever, A. Lincoln": How the Unlikely Friendship of Gustav Koerner and Abraham Lincoln Changed America Forever* (Gretna, LA: Pelican Publishing Company, forthcoming).

7. Jack Le Chien, *"We Must Make Them Understand Lincoln Is Our Man"* (Belleville, IL: Köerner House Restoration Committee, 2011), 5–6.

8. Abraham Lincoln to Gustave P. Koerner, July 25, 1858, *Collected Works*, 2:524. For a different perspective, see Charles Granville Hamilton, *Lincoln and the Know Nothing Movement* (Washington, DC: Public Affairs Press, 1954).

9. Lincoln, "Speech at Meredosia, Illinois," October 18, 1858, and Abraham Lincoln to Edward Lusk, October 30, 1858, *Collected Works*, 3:329, 333.

10. Lincoln, "Speech at Chicago, Illinois," July 10, 1858, ibid., 2:484–502.

11. Abraham Lincoln to Schuyler Colfax, July 6, 1859, ibid., 3:391.

12. *Chicago Press and Tribune*, March 21, 1859.

13. *Dubuque (IA) Daily Express and Herald*, May 25, 1859.

14. F. I. Herriot, *The Premises and Significance of Abraham Lincoln's Letter to Theodore Canisius* (1915; reprinted from *Deutsch-Amerikanische Geschichtsblätter Jahrbuch der Deutsch-Amerikanischen Historischen Gesellschaft*

von Illinois [*German-American History Yearbook of the German-American Historical Society of Illinois*] 15, 1915), 36–37, 57.

15. Abraham Lincoln to Theodore Canisius, May 17, 1859, *Collected Works*, 3:380; A. E. Zucker, "Dr. Theodore Canisius, Friend of Lincoln," *American-German Review* 16 (February 1950): 13–15, 38.

16. Herriot, *Premises and Significance*, 39–40.

17. James Cornelius, "Hopeful Hint of Future News(paper)," *From Out of the Top Hat: A Blog from the Abraham Lincoln Presidential Library and Museum*, August 30, 2011, http://www.alplm.org/blog/tag/theodore-canisius/.

18. Herriot, *Premises and Significance*, 57–58.

19. Reinhard H. Lutin, "Lincoln Appeals to German American Voters," *German-American Review* 25 (June–July 1959): 4–6, 15; Raymond Lohne, "Team of Friends: A New Lincoln Theory and Legacy," *Journal of the Illinois State Historical Society* 101 (Fall–Winter 2008): 40–46. See also Raymond A. Lohne, "Founded at the Bier of Lincoln: A History of the Germania Club of Chicago, 1865–1986" (PhD diss., University of Illinois at Chicago, 2007), 10–73.

20. Abraham Lincoln to Joshua F. Speed, August 24, 1855, *Collected Works*, 2:320–23.

21. Abraham Lincoln to Owen Lovejoy, August 11, 1855, ibid., 2:316–17.

22. Gustave Koerner to Abraham Lincoln, April 4, 1859, Robert Todd Lincoln Papers.

23. Abraham Lincoln to Mark W. Delahay, May 14, 1859, and Lincoln, "Speech at Clinton, Illinois," October 14, 1859, *Collected Works*, 3:378–79, 487–89.

24. John H. Bryant and Stephen G. Paddock to Abraham Lincoln, June 4, 1860, Robert Todd Lincoln Papers.

25. *New York Tribune*, April 26, 1859.

26. Abraham Lincoln to Theodore Canisius, May 17, 1859, *Collected Works*, 3:380.

27. Abraham Lincoln to James Berdan, July 10, 1856, ibid., 2:334–48.

28. Hamilton, *Lincoln and the Know Nothing Movement*, 3–12.

29. Stephen L. Hansen and Paul D. Nygard, "Abraham Lincoln and the Know Nothing Question, 1854–1859," *Lincoln Herald* 94 (Summer 1992): 61–72; Bruce Levine, "'The Vital Element of the Republican Party': Antislavery, Nativism, and Abraham Lincoln," *Journal of the Civil War Era* 1 (December 2011): 481–505.

30. *Leavenworth Daily Times*, September 4, 1858.

31. Ibid., November 28, 30, December 2, 3, 1859; Fred W. Brinkerhoff, "The Kansas Tour of Lincoln the Candidate," *Kansas History* 31 (Winter 2008–09): 275–93.

32. Lincoln, "Speech at Leavenworth, Kansas," December 3, 1859, and "Second Speech at Leavenworth, Kansas," December 5, 1859, *Collected Works*, 3:497–502, 502–4.

33. *Leavenworth Daily Times*, December 6, 1859.

34. *Marshall County Times*, November 24, 1859; *Sioux City Register*, December 2, 1859.

35. Abraham Lincoln to Schuyler Colfax, July 6, 1859, *Collected Works*, 3:391.

36. Carl Schurz Papers, General Correspondence, Manuscript Division, Library of Congress, Washington, DC; Alison Clark Efford, "Abraham Lincoln, German-Born Republicans, and American Citizenship," *Marquette Law Review* 93 (Winter 2010): 1375–81.

37. Andreas Dorpalen, "The German Element and the Issues of the Civil War," in *Ethnic Voters and the Election of Lincoln*, ed. Frederick C. Luebke (Lincoln: University of Nebraska Press, 1971), 68–91.

38. Howard K. Beale, ed., *The Diary of Edward Bates, 1859–1866* (New York: Da Capo Press, 1971), 129–31.

39. Carl Schurz to Abraham Lincoln May 22, 1860, Robert Todd Lincoln Papers.

40. Abraham Lincoln to Carl Schurz, June 18, 1860, *Collected Works*, 4:78–79; Anna Zafiris, "The Relationship between Carl Schurz and Abraham Lincoln" (seminar paper, Ruhr-Universität, Bochum, Munich], Germany: GRIN Verlag, 2003).

41. Frederick Bancroft, ed., *Speeches, Correspondence and Political Papers of Carl Schurz* (New York: McClure, 1907–1908), 1:79–107; Hans L. Trefousse, *Carl Schurz: A Biography* (Knoxville: University of Tennessee Press, 1982), 270–76.

42. Bancroft, *Carl Schurz*, 1:160–63.

43. James M. Bergquist, "People and Politics in Transition: The Illinois Germans, 1850–1860," in Luebke, *Ethnic Voters and the Election of Lincoln*, 196–226. Although a bit dated, this anthology includes a number of interesting and useful essays. A superb analysis of the election of 1860 can be found in William E. Gienapp, "Who Voted for Lincoln?," in *Abraham Lincoln and the American Political Tradition*, ed. John L. Thomas (Amherst: University of Massachusetts Press, 1986), 50–97.

44. Lincoln, "Speech to Germans at Cincinnati, Ohio," February 12, 1861, *Collected Works*, 4:201–3.

4. Wisdom: Whig in the White House

1. Lincoln, "Speech to Germans at Cincinnati, Ohio," February 12, 1862, *Collected Works*, 4:201–3.

2. "Lincoln's Blood German?," *New York Times*, May 29, 1910; George M. Stephenson, *A History of American Immigration, 1820–1924* (Boston: Ginn and Co., 1926), 132; Richard O'Connor, *The German-Americans: An Informal History* (Boston: Little, Brown, and Co., 1968), 132–36; Albert B. Faust, *The German Element in the United States* (Boston: Houghton Mifflin Co., 1909), 2:183–84n.

3. Thomas J. McCormick, *Memoirs of Gustave Koerner, 1809–96, Life Sketches Written at the Suggestion of His Children* (Cedar Rapids, IA: Torch Press, 1909), 2:61, 71–95, 112, 118.

4. Michael Burlingame, ed., *John Hay's Anonymous Writings for the Press, 1860–1864* (Carbondale: Southern Illinois University Press, 1998), 24.

5. Abraham Lincoln to William H. Seward, March 18, 1861, *Collected Works*, 4:292–93.

6. Carl Schurz to Abraham Lincoln, March 28, 1861, Abraham Lincoln Papers.

7. David Work, *Lincoln's Political Generals* (Urbana: University of Illinois Press, 2009), 21–22.

8. Carl Schurz, *The Reminiscences of Carl Schurz* (New York: McClure Company, 1908–09).

9. Abraham Lincoln to Carl Schurz, November 24, 1862, *Collected Works*, 5:509–10.

10. Reinhard H. Luthin, "Lincoln Appeals to German American Voters," *German-American Review* 25 (June–July 1959): 4–6, 15. Although dated, Harry J. Carman and Reinhard H. Luthin, *Lincoln and the Patronage* (New York: Columbia University Press, 1943) still has some very useful information.

11. Gustave Koerner to Abraham Lincoln, April 5, 1861, Abraham Lincoln Papers.

12. Theodore Smith, *The Life and Writings of James A. Garfield* (New Haven, CT: Yale University Press, 1925), 179; Harold E. Hammond, ed., *A Diary of a Union Lady, 1861–1865* (New York: Funk and Wagnalls, 1962), 247.

13. Stephen D. Engle, *Yankee Dutchman: The Life of Franz Sigel* (Fayetteville: University of Arkansas Press, 1993), 150–59.

14. Abraham Lincoln to Henry W. Halleck, January 15, 1862, *Collected Works*, 5:99–101.

15. Henry W. Halleck to Abraham Lincoln, January 21, 1862, Robert Todd Lincoln Papers.

16. Gustave Koerner to Abraham Lincoln, January 26, 1862, ibid.

17. Abraham Lincoln to John C. Frémont, September 2, 1861, *Collected Works*, 4:506–7; *Harper's Weekly*, September 28, 1861.

18. For a very interesting account of a German immigrant who literally walked in off the street to meet President Lincoln see Louis Hensel,

My Life in America Before, During and After the Civil War (New York: Jo-An Books, 2009), 129–35. After coming to America, Hensel worked a number of jobs before traveling with the German Opera Company of New York. Lincoln regularly attended the opera company's performances, and after one, he invited the crew to visit him at the White House. When Hensel could find no one else to join him in accepting Lincoln's invitation, he walked into the East Room of the White House on March 27, 1863, coincidentally with a delegation of representatives from the Cheyenne, Kiowa, Arapaho, Comanche, Apache, and Caddo tribes, and was mistaken for their interpreter. It is believed that his eyewitness report of that meeting has never been published before.

19. F. E. Leseure to Abraham Lincoln, July 26, 1860; N. M. Knapp to Abraham Lincoln, June 21, 1858; and Rhoda E. White to Abraham Lincoln, December 15, 1860, in David C. Mearns, ed., *The Lincoln Papers* (Garden City, NY: Doubleday and Company, 1948), 1:270–71, 209–10; 2:341–43.

20. *Boston Pilot*, October 13, 1860; *Irish News*, May 31, 1856.

21. *Boston Pilot*, October 13, 1860; *New York Tribune*, May 8, 1860.

22. Sidney Davis Brummer, *Political History of New York State during the Period of the Civil War* (1911; repr., New York: AMS Press, 1967), 326.

23. *New York Metropolitan Record*, February 14, November 20, 1863.

24. Benjamin J. Blied, *Catholics and the Civil War* (Milwaukee, 1945), 76–77.

25. Rena Mazyck Andrews, "Archbishop John Hughes and the Civil War" (PhD diss., University of Chicago, 1935), 15.

26. *New York Metropolitan Record*, February 13, March 12, 1864.

27. Smith, *Lincoln and the New Immigrant Irish*, 4.

28. William Shannon, *The American Irish: A Political and Social Portrait* (New York: Macmillan, 1963), 52–59.

29. William L. D. O'Grady, "Lincoln and the Irish Flag," letter to the editor of the *New York Herald*, February 12, 1917.

30. *New York Tribune*, July 18, 1863.

31. Abraham Lincoln to Horatio Seymour, August 7, 1863, *Collected Works*, 6:369–70.

32. Carl Wittke, *The Irish in America* (Baton Rouge: Louisiana State University Press, 1956), 140–47.

33. Lincoln, "Address before the Wisconsin State Agricultural Society, Milwaukee, Wisconsin," September 30, 1859, *Collected Works*, 3:471–82.

34. Harold Holzer, *Lincoln and the Jews: The Last Best Hope of Earth* (Los Angeles: Skirball Cultural Center, 2002), 5–6.

35. Lincoln, "Order for the Sabbath Observance," November 15, 1862, *Collected Works*, 5:497–98.

36. Abraham Lincoln to Arnold Fischel, December 14, 1861, ibid., 5:69. For an extremely interesting account of a Jewish Washington insider and his inconsistent relationship with Lincoln, see Esther L. Panitz, *Simon Wolf: Private Conscience and Public Image* (Rutherford, NJ: Fairleigh Dickinson University Press, 1987), especially pages 22–29.

37. *New York Herald*, October 3, 1862. Interestingly, in March 2013 researchers located the grave of Zacharie, who died in 1900. The discovery was made in Highgate Cemetery in London, not far from the final resting place of Karl Marx. *Camden New Journal*, February 26, 2013.

38. Isaac Markens, *Abraham Lincoln and the Jews* (New York: Publications of the American Jewish Historical Society, 1909), 58–59; Roy P. Basler, ed., *The Collected Works of Abraham Lincoln: Supplement, 1832–1865* (Westport, CT: Greenwood Press, 1974), 165n.

39. John Hay to Meyer Isaacs, November 1, 1864, Robert Todd Lincoln Papers.

40. Albert A. Woldman, "Lincoln's Jewish Doctor," *B'nai B'rith National Jewish Monthly*, February 1937, 189; Betram W. Korn, *American Jewry and the Civil War* (Philadelphia: The Jewish Publication Society, 1951), 197–203; Gary Phillip Zola, *"We Called Him Rabbi Abraham": Lincoln and American Jewry; A Documentary History* (Carbondale: Southern Illinois University Press, 2014), 44–138.

41. Korn, *American Jewry and the Civil War*, 121–55.

42. Jonathan D. Sarna, *When Grant Expelled the Jews* (New York: Schoken, 2012), 22; *Collected Works*, 6:71n.

43. Korn, *American Jewry and the Civil War*, 203; Sarna, *When Grant Expelled the Jews*, 20–23.

44. Naphtali J. Rubinger, *Abraham Lincoln and the Jews* (New York: Jonathan David Publishers, 1962), 42.

45. *The War of Rebellion: A Compilation of the Official Records of the Union and Confederate Armies* (Washington, DC: Government Printing Office, 1880–1901), ser. 3, vol. 2, 301.

46. John Fabian Witt, *Lincoln's Code: The Laws of War in American History* (New York: Free Press, 2012), 1–9.

47. Ibid., 193–95, 231–49, 347–53.

48. Mary D. Meyer, "The Germans in Wisconsin and the Civil War: Their Attitude toward the Union, the Republicans, Slavery, and Lincoln" (master's thesis, Catholic University of America, 1937), 45–46.

49. Lincoln, "Proclamation Concerning Aliens," May 8, 1863, *Collected Works*, 6:203–4.

50. Lincoln, "Annual Message to Congress," December 8, 1863, ibid., 7:36–53.

51. *Hardware Reporter*, December 1863, quoted in Albert Hess Leisinger Jr., "The Federal Act to Encourage Immigration, July 4, 1864" (master's thesis, Cornell University, 1938), 31. See also Heather Cox Richardson, *The Greatest Nation of the Earth: Republican Economic Policies during the Civil War* (Cambridge: Harvard University Press, 1997), 161–69.

52. "Federal Immigration Policies, 1864–1924," *University Journal of Business* 2 (March 1924): 133–56.

53. Leisinger, "Federal Act to Encourage Immigration," 45–51.

54. Lincoln, "Annual Message to Congress," December 6, 1864, *Collected Works*, 8:136–53.

55. Richard N. Current, ed., *The Political Thought of Abraham Lincoln* (Indianapolis: Bobbs-Merrill, 1967), xiii–xxxi.

5. Certainty: The Great Emancipator or the Great Egalitarian?

1. Allen T. Rice, ed., *Reminiscences of Abraham Lincoln by Distinguished Men of His Time* (New York: North American Review, 1886), 475; Lincoln, "Eulogy on Henry Clay," July 6, 1852, *Collected Works*, 2:121–32.

2. Lincoln, "Speech at Springfield, Illinois," June 26, 1857, *Collected Works*, 2:398–410.

3. Lincoln, "Speech at Chicago, Illinois," July 10, 1858, ibid., 2:484–502; Leiker, "Difficulties of Understanding Abe," 86.

4. Lincoln, "Fragment on Government," [July 1, 1854?], *Collected Works*, 2:221–22.

5. Lincoln, "Speech in the Illinois Legislature Concerning the State Bank," January 11, 1837, *Collected Works*, 1:61–69.

6. See Richard N. Current, *Union, Ethnicity, and Abraham Lincoln*, first annual R. Gerald McMurtry Lecture (Fort Wayne, IN: Louis A. Warren Lincoln Library and Museum, 1978); Lincoln, "Address before the Young Men's Lyceum of Springfield, Illinois," January 27, 1838, *Collected Works*, 1:108–15.

7. Lincoln, "Speech at Springfield, Illinois," June 26, 1857, ibid., 2:398–410.

8. Diggins, *On Hallowed Ground*, 28–31, 41–48.

9. Ibid., 48–49, 177–81.

10. Lincoln, "Speech at Peoria, Illinois," October 16, 1854, *Collected Works*, 2:247–83.

11. Lincoln, "Speech at New Haven, Connecticut," March 6, 1860, ibid., 4:30.

12. Lincoln, "Speech to the Germans at Cincinnati, Ohio," February 12, 1861, ibid., 4:201–3.

13. Lincoln, "Speech at Chicago, Illinois," July 10, 1858, ibid., 2:484–502.

14. Lincoln, "Speech in Independence Hall, Philadelphia, Pennsylvania," February 22, 1861, ibid., 4:240–41.

15. Lincoln, "Speech and Resolutions Concerning Philadelphia Riots," June 12, 1844, ibid., 1:337–38.
16. Lincoln, "To Owen Lovejoy," August 11, 1855, ibid., 2:316–17.
17. Wilson and Davis, *Herndon's Informants*, 705.
18. Lincoln, "Address before the Young Men's Lyceum of Springfield, Illinois," January 27, 1838, and "Communication to the People of Sangamo County," March 9, 1832, *Collected Works*, 1:108–15, 5–9.
19. Lincoln, "Reply to New York Workingmen's Democratic Republican Association," March 21, 1864, ibid., 7:259–60.
20. Diggins, *On Hallowed Ground*, 30.
21. Lincoln, "Address at Sanitary Fair, Baltimore, Maryland," April 18, 1864, *Collected Works*, 7:301–3.
22. Lincoln, "Speech at Springfield, Illinois," June 26, 1857, ibid., 2:398–410.
23. Lincoln, "To John McMahon," August 6, 1864, ibid., 7:483; LaWanda Cox, *Lincoln and Black Freedom* (Columbia: University of South Carolina Press, 1981), 25.

INDEX

Italicized page numbers indicate figures.

Jason H. Silverman is the Ellison Capers Palmer Jr. Professor of History at Winthrop University. He is the author or editor of ten other books, including *Unwelcome Guests*, *Shanks*, and *A Rising Star of Promise*. He is a former South Carolina Governor's Professor of the Year.

CONCISE
LINCOLN
LIBRARY

This series of concise books fills a need for short studies of the life, times, and legacy of President Abraham Lincoln. Each book gives readers the opportunity to quickly achieve basic knowledge of a Lincoln-related topic. These books bring fresh perspectives to well-known topics, investigate previously overlooked subjects, and explore in greater depth topics that have not yet received book-length treatment. For a complete list of current and forthcoming titles, see www.conciselincolnlibrary.com.

Other Books in the Concise Lincoln Library

*Abraham Lincoln and
Horace Greeley*
Gregory A. Borchard

Lincoln and the Civil War
Michael Burlingame

Lincoln and the Constitution
Brian R. Dirck

*Lincoln and the Election
of 1860*
Michael S. Green

Lincoln and the Union Governors
William C. Harris

Lincoln's Campaign Biographies
Thomas A. Horrocks

Lincoln and the Military
John F. Marszalek

Lincoln and Emancipation
Edna Greene Medford

Lincoln and Reconstruction
John C. Rodrigue

*Lincoln and the Thirteenth
Amendment*
Christian G. Samito

Lincoln and Medicine
Glenna R. Schroeder-Lein

Lincoln and the U.S. Colored Troops
John David Smith

Lincoln's Assassination
Edward Steers, Jr.

Lincoln and Race
Richard Striner

Lincoln and Religion
Ferenc Morton Szasz with
Margaret Connell Szasz

Lincoln and the War's End
John C. Waugh

Lincoln as Hero
Frank J. Williams

Abraham and Mary Lincoln
Kenneth J. Winkle